I Am Not Your Negro

As the inaugural volume in the Docalogue series, this book models a new form for the discussion of documentary film.

James Baldwin's writing is intensely relevant to contemporary politics and culture, and Peck's strategies for representing him and conveying his work in *I Am Not Your Negro* (2016) raise important questions about how documentary can bring the work of a complex thinker like Baldwin to a broader public. By combining five distinct perspectives on a single documentary film, this book offers different critical approaches to the same media object, acting both as an intensive scholarly treatment of a film and as a guide for how to analyze, theorize, and contextualize a documentary.

Undergraduate and graduate students as well as scholars of film and media studies, communication studies, African American studies, and gender and sexuality studies will find this book extremely useful in understanding the significance of this film and the ways in which it offers insight into not only Baldwin and his writings but also wider historical and contemporary realities.

Jaimie Baron is Associate Professor of Film Studies at the University of Alberta. She is the author of *The Archive Effect: Found Footage and the Audiovisual Experience of History* (2014) and *Reuse, Misuse, Abuse: The Ethics of Audiovisual Appropriation in the Digital Era* (2020) as well as many journal articles and book chapters. She is also the founder, director, and co-curator of the Festival of (In)appropriation, a yearly international festival of short experimental found footage films and videos.

Kristen Fuhs is Associate Professor of Media Studies in the Department of Communication at Woodbury University. She writes about documentary film, the American criminal justice system, and contemporary celebrity, and her work has appeared in journals such as *Cultural Studies*; the *Historical Journal of Film, Radio, and Television*; and the *Journal of Sport & Social Issues*.

Docalogue
Series Editors: Jaimie Baron and Kristen Fuhs

Each book in the Docalogue book series highlights a recent documentary film from five different scholarly perspectives. By focusing on a single documentary from multiple points of view, each book demonstrates the ways in which a single film can open onto diverse questions having to do with the status of the "real," documentary ethics, and the politics of representation, among other issues. The book series is an extension of Docalogue.com, a monthly online publication that consists of short essays about contemporary documentary films.

I Am Not Your Negro
A Docalogue
Edited by Jaimie Baron and Kristen Fuhs

For more information on the series, visit: https://www.routledge.com/Docalogue/book-series/DOCALOGUE

I Am Not Your Negro
A Docalogue

Edited by Jaimie Baron and
Kristen Fuhs

DOCALOGUE

First published 2021
by Routledge
2 Park Square, Milton Park, Abingdon, Oxon OX14 4RN

and by Routledge
52 Vanderbilt Avenue, New York, NY 10017

Routledge is an imprint of the Taylor & Francis Group, an informa business

© 2021 selection and editorial matter, Jaimie Baron and Kristen Fuhs; individual chapters, the contributors

The right of Jaimie Baron and Kristen Fuhs to be identified as the authors of the editorial material, and of the authors for their individual chapters, has been asserted in accordance with sections 77 and 78 of the Copyright, Designs and Patents Act 1988.

All rights reserved. No part of this book may be reprinted or reproduced or utilised in any form or by any electronic, mechanical, or other means, now known or hereafter invented, including photocopying and recording, or in any information storage or retrieval system, without permission in writing from the publishers.

Trademark notice: Product or corporate names may be trademarks or registered trademarks, and are used only for identification and explanation without intent to infringe.

British Library Cataloguing-in-Publication Data
A catalogue record for this book is available from the British Library

Library of Congress Cataloging-in-Publication Data
Names: Baron, Jaimie, editor. | Fuhs, Kristen, editor.
Title: I am not your Negro: a docalogue / edited by Jaimie Baron and Kristen Fuhs.
Description: London; New York: Routledge, 2020. |
Series: Docalogue | Includes bibliographical references and index.
Identifiers: LCCN 2020014563 (print) | LCCN 2020014564 (ebook) | ISBN 9780367178949 (hardback) | ISBN 9780429058301 (ebook)
Subjects: LCSH: United States—Race relations. | I am not your Negro (Motion picture). | Documentary films—United States. | Civil rights movements—United States—History—20th century. | Racism—United States. | African Americans—Civil rights—History—20th century.
Classification: LCC E185.61 .I15 2020 (print) | LCC E185.61 (ebook) | DDC 305.800973—dc23
LC record available at https://lccn.loc.gov/2020014563
LC ebook record available at https://lccn.loc.gov/2020014564

ISBN: 978-0-367-17894-9 (hbk)
ISBN: 978-0-367-52312-1 (pbk)
ISBN: 978-0-429-05830-1 (ebk)

Typeset in Bembo
by codeMantra

Visit the companion website: www.docalogue.com.

Contents

List of figures vii
Preface viii

Introduction: the timeliness of *I Am Not Your Negro* 1
JAIMIE BARON

1 *I Am Not Your Negro*'s queer poetics of identity and omission 9
COURTNEY R. BAKER

2 James Baldwin's embodied absence: *I Am Not Your Negro* and filmic corporeality 24
LAURA RASCAROLI

3 "Some One of Us Should Have Been There with Her": gender, race, and sexuality in *I Am Not Your Negro* and contemporary Black experimental documentary 38
ELLEN C. SCOTT

4 James Baldwin: *The Price of the Ticket* (1989) and *I Am Not Your Negro* (2016) as historicist documentaries 52
STEPHEN CASMIER

5   **Techniques for truth-telling from *Haitian
    Corner* to *I Am Not Your Negro*** 72
    TONI PRESSLEY-SANON

Bibliography 87
Filmography 93
Contributor biographies 95
Index 97

Figures

1.1 Sidney Poitier as Virgil Tibbs in *In the Heat of the Night* (Norman Jewison, 1967) — 20
1.2 Rod Steiger as Sheriff Gillespie in *In the Heat of the Night* (Norman Jewison, 1967) — 20
2.1 Incarnate screen: *The Gospel According to St. Matthew (Il Vangelo secondo Matteo*, 1964) projected onto the torso of its director, Pier Paolo Pasolini, during the performance *Intellettuale* (Fabio Mauri, 13 May 1975). Photo: Antonio Masotti/Cineteca di Bologna — 25
2.2 James Baldwin invokes a phantasmatic racialized projection onto his body during a televised debate. *I Am Not Your Negro* (Raoul Peck, 2016) — 33
3.1 *Strong Island* (Yance Ford, 2017) — 45
3.2 *Lorraine Hansberry: Sighted Eyes/Feeling Heart* (Tracey Heather Strain, 2017) — 46
4.1 Cosmopolitan Baldwin, *James Baldwin: The Price of the Ticket* (Karen Thorsen, 1989) — 58
4.2 Prophetic Baldwin, *I Am Not Your Negro* (Raoul Peck, 2016) — 63
5.1 James Baldwin and Dick Cavett on *The Dick Cavett Show* in *I Am Not Your Negro* (Raoul Peck, 2016) — 75
5.2 Tableau of men and women of African descent in *I Am Not Your Negro* (Raoul Peck, 2016) — 82

Preface

Docalogue began in 2017 – and continues – as an online journal, but it also began as a documentary salon in Los Angeles a decade earlier when the editors were both graduate students. Each month, we and a number of friends and colleagues would meet at one of our homes to watch and discuss a documentary film. Although the salon only lasted a year or so, it was one of the most stimulating forums for discussion of documentary film that we experienced during our graduate years. When the editors each moved on to academic jobs in different cities, we continued to meet at conferences, particularly Visible Evidence, which provides a major forum for documentary screening and discussion. Although Visible Evidence is always exciting and generative, we longed to have a way to sustain our discussions of documentary media throughout the year. From this desire arose Docalogue, a digital publication wherein we select one recent documentary each month and solicit two scholars to write a short essay about it, offering two perspectives intended to start off a broader conversation, whether on the website, in classrooms, or within documentary scholarship more broadly.

After about a year of provocative posts in this form, we decided that we might expand the Docalogue format to include short, edited books offering multiple perspectives on a single documentary film – a format that had rarely been tried, at least for nonfiction media. One of the challenges we have faced is how to decide which documentaries to choose as subjects of book-length study. On the website, this is less pressing since we feature so many documentaries, and the purpose is simply to foster scholarly conversation. In choosing documentaries for the book series, however, we are by definition singling out particular documentaries that we think have more than passing significance. And, since our focus is recent documentaries, this is necessarily a gamble: we do not know for certain which films will stand the test of time. In addition, while our aim is not to establish a new canon, by virtue of focusing a whole book on a film, we cannot help but raise the profile of the film at least within the documentary scholarly community. In the end, we decided to take the risk and simply choose films that we believe raise important issues about documentary in the contemporary moment and open themselves up to multiple avenues of scholarly analysis. Moreover, our aim is also to center at least some films that emerge from makers whose voices have not always been foregrounded by documentary scholarship.

The purpose of the Docalogue book series is, however, not to close the book, as it were, on any film. The idea is to open up conversation among scholars, to demonstrate to students the many ways of approaching a documentary text, and to offer a resource for those who wish to teach recent documentary films about which little has been written so far. We hope that, like the online journal, the book series will give rise to further scholarship about the films in question.

We would like to thank our Board of Advisors – Chris Cagle, Timothy Corrigan, Oliver Gaycken, Maria Pramaggiore, Pooja Rangan, Mila Turajlić, and Janet Walker – for their advice and suggestions regarding the selection of films and writers. We also thank our reviewers – Timothy Corrigan, Alisa Lebow, and Seth Feldman – for their feedback on both our series proposal and this book. Our gratitude also goes out to all of the writers who have contributed thus far to the Docalogue project and to our editor at Routledge, Natalie Foster, for supporting this series.

For more information about the Docalogue website, go to www.docalogue.com.

Introduction

The timeliness of *I Am Not Your Negro*

Jaimie Baron

There is a certain irony in the title of Raoul Peck's 2017 film based on the work of James Baldwin. "The title would have been even more percussive," critic Herb Boyd writes, "if the n-word were substituted for Negro, which Baldwin often did."[1] Of course, in the contemporary moment, Peck absolutely could not use the n-word that Baldwin frequently used precisely in order to question and deconstruct its power. Had Peck included the n-word in his title, *I Am Not Your Negro* would never have been nominated for an Academy Award. Indeed, it would never have been released. The title thus reflects our paradoxical moment when the n-word cannot be uttered in polite liberal company, but racist police continue to brutalize and kill African Americans in the streets, even on video, and be acquitted of any crime. Baldwin himself would likely have had something quite incisive to say about the timidity of those who would fight racism by demonizing a set of offensive phonemes while limiting their activism to posting social media rants in response to videos of Black people being murdered in cold blood. He might also have had some cutting remarks about the 2019 incident at Augsburg University in Minnesota in which a white professor was suspended for uttering the n-word aloud in class in the context of discussing its use in Baldwin's book *The Fire Next Time* (1963) – while a friend of unabashed white supremacists sits in the Oval Office.[2] We will, of course, never know what Baldwin would say about the Trump era, and few, if any, contemporary figures can match Baldwin's eloquent, erudite rage. Given that fact, then, it makes sense to call upon the dead man himself to speak to us from beyond the grave.

I Am Not Your Negro was one of the most discussed documentaries of 2017. Although it lost the Academy Award for Best Documentary Feature to Ezra Edelman and Caroline Waterlow's five-part television documentary *OJ: Made in America*, it generated just as much, if not more, debate about contemporary race relations in America as did the

Oscar-winning film. Reviews of the film consistently emphasized its timeliness. As film critic A.O. Scott put it,

> Though its principal figure, the novelist, playwright and essayist James Baldwin, is a man who has been dead for nearly 30 years, you would be hard-pressed to find a movie that speaks to the present moment with greater clarity and force, insisting on uncomfortable truths and drawing stark lessons from the shadows of history.[3]

Scott further noted the ways in which Baldwin's spoken words and writings speak with great prescience to the moment that gave rise to the Black Lives Matter movement, in which white supremacy has been once again revealed in all of its structural and material power. In a similar vein, Warren Crichlow writes,

> Addressing 1960's America, [Peck] simultaneously issues dispatches to contemporary audiences, parlaying past tragic events and their voiced aftermath into the present, for they so uncannily resemble present-day circumstances, both social and political. This time-space compression effect mesmerizes, as Peck takes Baldwin's lead, inexorably linking epochs and generations of experience.[4]

This mesmerizing sense of time-space compression is perhaps what is most striking about this film. Repurposing dated archival footage always produces a sense of past meeting present, but channeled through Peck's selections and editing, Baldwin seems to be speaking directly to the present moment, as if he were still alive, watching and considering us from beyond the screen.

This sense of timeliness applies not only to Peck's film but to Baldwin's work in general. Indeed, the recent renewed interest in Baldwin's writings as a whole points to the ways in which the postracial fantasy expressed in certain circles during Barack Obama's presidency never coincided with reality. Crichlow notes that "Over the last twenty years, reappraisal and an animated critical rethinking of Baldwin's life and work in scholarly circles have reached a pinnacle of activity, culminating perhaps in the year-long interdisciplinary celebration of Baldwin's ninetieth birthday in 2014."[5] The establishment of the recurring International James Baldwin Conference and the open access journal *James Baldwin Review* and numerous new books published about Baldwin and his works point to the way in which this interest is hardly on the wane. The aptly titled collection *James Baldwin Now* (though published back in 1999) attempted to theorize

Baldwin's continuing relevance – even before the elections of Barack Obama and Donald Trump, which arguably increased it further. The more recent release of *If Beale Street Could Talk*, Barry Jenkins' 2018 adaptation of Baldwin's novel of the same name, also attests to a popular interest in Baldwin's writings now.

But what, precisely, do we mean by "timeliness"? Lee Carruthers has noted that "When we refer to something as 'timely' we mean that it comes at a moment that is suitable: a timely action, for instance, is one that is appropriate or relevant for our present situation."[6] Baldwin's writings are thus timely in the sense that they seem to describe what is happening in our society now as well as at the time they were written. This ascription of timeliness to *I Am Not Your Negro* emphasizes the ways in which social relations and racial politics have not changed – or have changed much less than we might like to think. Yet, Andrew Chan warns against this sense of timeliness in relation to Peck's film and to Baldwin's work as a whole, writing,

> The great risk of applying Baldwin's words to our present-day horrors is that it lends his work an undue semblance of prophecy. But Baldwin was no clairvoyant, and this false projection only allows us to interpret the persistence of injustice as somehow inevitable, deflecting our collective responsibility to eradicate the ills he diagnosed. When we listen to Baldwin disassemble the logic of racism, as this film gives us ample chance to do, we are responding not to the man's foresight but to his courage to speak from within the specificity of his own time and place.[7]

Thus, the experience of timeliness may have multiple implications. It allows us to see the connections between past and present anew and to recognize, despite what we might want to believe, how little has changed; and this seems an important revelation. At the same time, however, it potentially allows us to shrug off our responsibility for these continuities and to deny the specificities of particular historical moments. There is, perhaps, a pleasure inherent in the feeling of timeliness, in the sense that Baldwin is clairvoyant, but this pleasure may also be accompanied by disavowal, of feeling like the wrongs of the present are not our fault since it has "always been this way." Indeed, the feeling of recognition – even of Freudian repetition – may hold pleasure in itself. We like to see ourselves – our moment – reflected, even if in a negative light.

Carruthers, however, also suggests a more phenomenological understanding of cinematic timeliness that foregrounds the viewer's temporal experience while watching a film: "Attending to the timeliness of cinematic time is to undertake an analysis of film's temporal rhetorics, so as to offer a rich account of the experience that they generate."[8] This makes particular sense in relation to a film about Baldwin, whose own film analyses were intertwined with his personal experiences. As Chan puts it,

> For Baldwin, cinema opens the mind up to a kind of free-associative soul-searching. The experience of a film lives at the intersection between an entrancing, dreamlike medium and each viewer's own incoherent repository of hopes, fears, memories, and moral convictions.[9]

Thus, it follows that we should attend to our intersecting experiences of historical time, cinematic time, and individual time when watching a film about Baldwin, who deftly eludes any attempt to secure him in the safely historical past. And I would argue that the very timeliness of *I Am Not Your Negro* – in both senses I have described – has immediate implications for us as viewers and as (historical) agents.

Several scholars, including Crichlow, have referred to *I Am Not Your Negro* as an essay film and have lauded Peck for the ways in which he assembled archival fragments – both written and audiovisual – in order to produce a renewed understanding of Baldwin's life and work. Crichlow has noted that "While the archival footage utilized in *I Am Not Your Negro* might be familiar to any serious student of Baldwin, it is the scrupulous and uncanny way actuality footage is re-assembled that constitutes this film's singular experience."[10] This actuality footage includes Baldwin's 1965 television debate with William F. Buckley, his 1968 appearance on *The Dick Cavett Show*, footage from Horace Ové's 1968 film about Baldwin (whose title *did* include the n-word), and excerpts from Richard O. Moore's 1963 documentary *Take This Hammer*. Beyond this juxtaposition of archival footage from multiple moments, the specific temporality of the essay film has crucial implications for questions of the viewer's agency and, hence, responsibility. Timothy Corrigan writes that one might characterize the essay film as a means of intervening in "the reporting of past, present, and future facts and events in a fashion that tends to blend and blur those three registers as 'current events'."[11] The timeliness described by critics above, then, is perhaps to some degree ingrained in the form of the essay film, which blurs distinct time periods in order to reveal their imbrication with one another. In contrast to Chan, Corrigan does not see this aspect of the essay film as an opportunity for abdication of responsibility by the viewer or an assessment of inevitability; in fact, he argues quite the opposite, suggesting that "the essayistic works to create the unsettling state in which the subject recognizes himself or herself, often uncomfortably, as a participant in the configuration that is the news and its history."[12] Indeed, he further suggests that the essay film "aims not only to activate a thinking subject before that empty screen but also to propel that thinking as an intellectual and concrete action within the historical unfolding of events."[13] Corrigan implies that precisely by not allowing the past to be clearly delineated from the present, the essay film hails us as responsible agents. Perhaps, then, the pleasure in the timeliness of *I Am Not Your Negro* is not simply that of recognition and repetition but also of an opportunity to intervene in the continuing unfolding of history, revealed (again) as continually unjust. Confronted with archival evidence of the ways in which Baldwin's assessments of his own historical moment resonate with ours, we are given a chance to locate ourselves within this broader temporal expanse and, ideally, to actively produce a different future, a future in which Baldwin's words will *not* resonate.

This desire for intervention is one reason that we have decided to inaugurate the Docalogue book series with this film. The name "Docalogue," of course, combines the words "documentary" and "-logue," meaning spoken or written discourse. The purpose of the series is to bring together multiple voices around a single documentary film as a means of both polyvocal theorization and active intervention. In addition to producing valuable discussion, we want to ask, what can documentary propel us to *do*? To acknowledge the timeliness of *I Am Not Your Negro* is also to assume responsibility for this time, a time in which scholars have an ethical obligation to intervene in the social structures that perpetuate discrimination, violence, injustice, poverty, environmental destruction, and so on.

Peck's film ends with Baldwin saying,

> If I'm not the n----- here and you invented him, you the white people invented him, then you've got to find out why. And the future of the country depends on that, whether or not it is able to ask that question.

This clip is, in fact, from 1963, one of the earlier clips of Baldwin included in the film. Reading this ending, Dan Sinykin notes,

> Peck's film spares its audience the full weight of Baldwin's apocalypticism… Baldwin, in leaving this future open, holds out a slim hope for resolution. But to find a Baldwin even this sanguine, Peck had to return to footage from 1963.[14]

Later in his life, Sinykin argues, Baldwin "resigns himself to being a witness to the apocalypse."[15] The essayistic temporality of Peck's film, however – with its recursive entanglement of past, present, and future – is incompatible with a linear, apocalyptic trajectory. By ending with Baldwin's words of 1963, Peck's film leaves us hovering in a moment of unresolved possibility. Apocalyptic time envisions an endpoint without hope. Although it may very well be on the horizon, the scholarly project demands that we – like Peck's film – suspend our belief in that end. In this spirit, this collection seeks to place multiple frames around Peck's film in order to provoke further speech, further discussion, and further action.

Courtney R. Baker's essay "*I Am Not Your Negro*'s Queer Poetics of Identity and Omission," starts off the collection by examining the film as a "writerly text" that refuses to reduce its materials to any singular or final meaning. Baker suggests that Peck lets the omissions and obfuscations of the archive retain their silence, compelling the film to contemplate its own desires and limitations. Her chapter outlines the formal features of Peck's mode of addressing absences and, despite the film's elision of Baldwin's queer identity, theorizes them as a form of queer poetics.

Next, in her essay "James Baldwin's Embodied Absence: *I Am Not Your Negro* and Filmic Corporeality," Laura Rascaroli approaches the film through questions of embodiment and invisibility, focusing on both Baldwin's absent body in much of the film and the effacement of Black bodies in American discourse more generally. She argues that *I Am Not Your Negro*'s narrative and aesthetic strategies – and particularly its use of archival materials – reflect the paradoxical ways in which the Black body is constantly and simultaneously both imaged and negated.

Ellen C. Scott's essay, "'Some One of Us Should Have Been There with Her': Gender, Race, and Sexuality in *I Am Not Your Negro* and Contemporary Black Experimental Documentary," brings into focus questions of gender in relation to both Baldwin's work and Peck's representation of Baldwin. She argues that Peck's version of Baldwin's Black voice partially replicates the 1960s' definition of public, respectable blackness as male. As a result, women – particularly Black women – are largely excluded from the film, along with queer subjects. Scott seeks to remedy this exclusion by placing Peck's film in dialogue with other recent, more intersectional documentary representations of blackness.

In "*James Baldwin: The Price of the Ticket* (1989) and *I Am Not Your Negro* (2016) as Historicist Documentaries," Stephen Casmier examines *I Am Not Your Negro* in relation to another documentary film about James Baldwin produced by Karen Thorsen in 1989. Through the conceptual lens of historicism, Casmier argues that both films use Baldwin's mid-century thoughts and persona to explore some of the most contentious discussions of their own moments of production. While *The Price of the Ticket* "recovers" Baldwin, who had been largely derided by the younger generation of Black activists, as a gay icon of 1980s identity politics, *I Am Not Your Negro* puts forth an image of Baldwin as a more radical figure, speaking to the needs of contemporary Black politics. Beyond this kind of "recovery," however, Casmier further suggests that Peck's film ultimately reclaims Baldwin as part of broader discourse of Black Atlantic and Haitian cosmology.

Finally, in "Techniques for Truth-Telling from *Haitian Corner* to *I Am Not Your Negro*," Toni Pressley-Sanon examines *I Am Not Your Negro* within the context of filmmaker Raoul Peck's career which is, in turn, part of a long tradition of artist-activist-scholars whose work bears witness to injustice of all kinds. She defines and examines a set of "truth-telling techniques" that Peck has deployed throughout his oeuvre with the aim of speaking truth to power, revealing previously "untenable" truths, and building a more just world for all.

It is our hope that this docalogue will be only the beginning of the discussion.

Notes

1 Herb Boyd, "*I Am Not Your Negro*," *Cineaste* 42, no. 2 (Spring 2017): 47.
2 See Colleen Flaherty, "Too Taboo for Class?" *Inside Higher Education*, 1 February 2019, www.insidehighered.com/news/2019/02/01/professor-suspended-using-n-word-class-discussion-language-james-baldwin-essay and Randall Kennedy, "How a Dispute Over the N-Word Became a Dispiriting Farce," *The Chronicle of Higher Education*, 8 February 2019, www.chronicle.com/article/How-a-Dispute-Over-the-N-Word/245655.
3 A.O. Scott, "'I Am Not Your Negro' Will Make You Rethink Race," *The New York Times*, 2 February 2017, C1.
4 Warren Crichlow, "Baldwin's Rendezvous with the Twenty-First Century: *I Am Not Your Negro*," *Film Quarterly* 70, no. 4 (Summer 2017): 11.
5 Crichlow, "Baldwin's Rendezvous," 17.
6 Lee Carruthers, "M. Bazin et le temps: Reclaiming the Timeliness of Cinematic Time," *Screen* 52, no. 1 (Spring 2011): 26.
7 Andrew Chan, "The Great Divide," *Film Comment* 53, no. 1 (January/February 2017): 58.
8 Carruthers, "M. Bazin et le temps," 27–28.
9 Chan, "The Great Divide," 56.
10 Crichlow, "Baldwin's Rendezvous," 10.

11 Timothy Corrigan, *The Essay Film: From Montaigne, after Marker* (Oxford: Oxford University Press, 2011), 154.
12 Corrigan, *The Essay Film*, 156.
13 Corrigan, *The Essay Film*, 164.
14 Dan Sinykin, "The Apocalyptic Baldwin," *Dissent* 64, no. 3 (Summer 2017): 18.
15 Sinykin, "The Apocalyptic Baldwin," 18.

1 *I Am Not Your Negro*'s queer poetics of identity and omission

Courtney R. Baker

I Am Not Your Negro is a cinematic journey, prompted by its subject's quest to make sense of his life in the wake of three earth-shattering deaths. As James Baldwin narrates his friendship with and admiration of the civil rights leaders Medgar Evers, Malcolm X, and Martin Luther King, Jr., the film explores Baldwin's relationship to the current conditions of blackness in the United States which have been informed by the legacies left by all four of those men. Authorized by Baldwin's unfinished manuscript, the film plays with time and the utterance to supply a complex but necessary study of the relationship between identity and history.

While the film does not announce itself to be particularly invested in Baldwin's queerness or even in the more expansive albeit academic discursivity of "queer Baldwin,"[1] it nevertheless adopts what might be termed a queer cinema poetics to reflect the fluidity of Baldwin's thoughts and writings. These poetics, rooted in the cinematic vocabulary of the shot and the cut, supply a dynamic, radically unbounded vision of US race relations as they play out on screen. Attending to but not determined by historical events, *I Am Not Your Negro* cruises the dystopia of American antiblackness in order to reflect upon Baldwin's insights on race, selfhood, and cinema.[2] Through a resistance to stasis and a commitment to movements both political and temporal, the film structurally embodies principles of radical progressiveness.

Whereas the film foregrounds director Raoul Peck's processing of Baldwin, resulting in the cinematic text known as *I Am Not Your Negro*, a critique of the film may itself be regarded as yet another layer of processing – this time by the spectator – which in turn produces yet another text, this time comprised of the spectator's encounter with the film text – itself comprised of a unique encounter between the filmmaker and the subject, James Baldwin. Though claims that a documentary reveals more about the filmmaker than the ostensible subject are not uncommon assertions, *I Am Not Your Negro* provides an especially compelling object of examination precisely because it foregrounds its constructedness and the labor entailed in the production of meaning. It is a film that allows its seams to show.

As a film project sourced from Baldwin's literary archives, the film necessarily employs a retrospective gaze but also makes an effort to trouble the presumed certitude of such a gesture. Indeed, it adopts a perspective akin to that presented in Peck's earlier film, *Lumumba: Death of Prophet* (1990), in which absences and aporias are permitted to resonate and in turn offer the viewer moments in which to reflect and to mourn. These moments of absence mark the places where the past touches the present but is not fully brought into it. These scenes, themselves characterized by abstract depictions of modern urban movement (literally planes, trains, and automobiles), bridge temporal moments but resist filling them. Instead, they return the viewer to watching time unfold and in so doing invite the viewer to interrogate the certainties of the past, of the present, and even of identity itself.

In the introduction to the book accompaniment to *I Am Not Your Negro*, Peck describes the importance of Baldwin's prose to his own self-knowledge as a Black man in the West. Baldwin was one of a handful of authors who "were telling stories describing history and defining structures and human relationships that matched what I was seeing around me."[3] This emphasis upon the interconnection of "history" and "structure" made sensible through "stories" invites a post-structuralist interpretation of Peck's meaning-making project, then and now, in which the power of discourse and language are foregrounded in a relation of non-dominance to either history or the present. Considering how C.L.R. James and Michel Foucault theorize the ordering of historical events for uses in the present illuminates the ways that Peck's films convey meaning. Specifically, Foucault's rejection of histories "of tradition and invention" in favor of a "history of ideas" that denotes a "history of perpetual difference" clarifies how an historiographic work, including a film, might emphasize invention rather than fixed knowledge of the past and future.[4] Similarly, C.L.R. James's figuration of the strategically suppressed accounting of the Haitian Revolution as a recoverable lever in the war against global fascism casts the history and the archive as undetermined but powerful sources of and for the present.[5]

Peck presents *I Am Not Your Negro* as a deeply personal film – not quite a hagiography but a sort of open letter in which the maker acknowledges his and our indebtedness to an author who is out of reach. While the author's individual biography is no determinant of meaning, one may consider how the film circulates alongside French and Francophone Caribbean philosophies of language and the self. Indeed, Peck, who is Haitian by birth, describes his childhood self as "inhabiting a myth in which I was both enforcer and actor" – a description that resonates with both French theorist Roland Barthes's notion of the cultural myth – the enabling but also restrictive system through which meanings are circulated – and Martiniquan psychoanalyst Franz Fanon's crushing self-awareness as the mythological Negro of cosmopolitan French fantasies.[6]

Following another post-structuralist thread laid down by Barthes's philosophies of language and literature, one perceives *I Am Not Your Negro* – as well as *Lumumba* – to be "writerly texts" that reject as false the notion that a complete(d) film is a closed text. To the contrary,

> [t]he writerly text is a perpetual present, upon which no *consequent* language (which would inevitably make it past) can be superimposed; the writerly text is *ourselves writing*, before the infinite play of the world (the world as function) is traversed, intersected, stopped, plasticized by some singular system (Ideology, Genus, Criticism) which reduces the plurality of entrances, the opening of networks, the infinity of languages.[7]

The stoppages of ideology et alia are resisted in the film conceptually by responding to Baldwin's own writerly prose as such, "disseminating it, ... dispersing it within the field of infinite difference."[8] Denying fixity in favor of dissemination and difference, *I Am Not Your Negro* embraces what Fred Moten describes as the poetics of the break and the atemporal "wherein black radicalism is set to work ... as part of a critique immanent to the black radical tradition that constitutes its radicalism as a cutting and abundant refusal of closure."[9] The film formally establishes its commitment to this tradition through both the cut and scenes of movement. These cinematic poetics work through and on the historical events referenced in Baldwin's writings (the murders of Evers, X, and King) and in our more recently passed moments of antiblack conflagrations (the Ferguson uprising and the murders of Tamir Rice, Walter Scott, and too many others). As in *Lumumba*, the film strives to reconstruct sense for our current moment out of the archive's abundances as well as from its prior, insufficient stories and the nonsense of history's aporias.

Following the opening sequence – a riot of stillness and motion and words comprised of Baldwin's calm but pessimistic appearance on *The Dick Cavett Show* in 1968 and a montage of photographs of the Ferguson uprising of 2015 accompanied by Buddy Guy's rollicking blues number, "Damn Right, I've Got the Blues" – the film returns to stark white text on a black background. Modernist, almost futurist animation announces the film as "Written by James Baldwin" and "Directed by Raoul Peck." With these words, *I Am Not Your Negro* announces itself as a collaboration afforded by a medium that can transgress the boundaries of death itself. The film, through its recruitment of visual, aural, and written records, operates as a spiritualist medium, echoing the wisdom of the past in the scenes of today.

The sequence that follows the titles reinforces the movement and shuttling between the past and the present that characterize this project. The narrator's voice, supplied by actor Samuel L. Jackson, breaks into the silence, announcing, "To Jay Acton." These words reflect the text of a source letter of Baldwin's written to his literary agent. Within moments, white letters mimicking typewriter script appear on a black screen, punctuated by the sound of tapping typewriter keys. The voice and the images on screen reinforce the moment of our viewing time and of Peck's directorial time; yet the words themselves reference the time of Baldwin's composition: June 30, 1979 to be exact. A past moment is reenacted in the moment of its passing in this scene.

In the letter and in the larger project of "Remember This House," Baldwin expresses the uncertainty about identity and direction that the film mirrors in its imagery and sounds. Baldwin's letter to Acton references the author's "divided mind" and the woeful sense that "[t]he summer has scarcely begun, and I feel, already, that it's almost over." Baldwin's letter goes on to announce his impending birthday and the commencement of a journey, one that Baldwin explains, "I always knew that I would have to make, but had hoped … not to have to make it so soon." Despite the felt inevitability of the journey, Baldwin remarks that the character of such a journey is itself, by nature, unknowable: "I am saying that a journey is called that because you cannot know what you will discover on the journey, what you will do with what you find, or what you find will do to you."[10] In the context of the film, with the words spoken by Jackson and visualized by Peck, the "I" – as well as the "you" – for whom these logics cohere is multiplied, generating multiple journeys for multiple addressors and addressees.

In this early scene, the film plays with the grammatical logic of its title, resisting not only the possessiveness of the words "your Negro" but also the inevitable belatedness and accuracy of the words "I am not." Certainly and sadly, James Baldwin is no longer, yet the film and the title articulate, seemingly despite themselves, a desire to return to the moment when the "I" could be located, assuredly, in the body of

Baldwin himself. As in *Lumumba*, following shots of train tracks, cars viewed hazily through a rain-soaked window, and tracking shots of landscapes as though viewed through a car or train window signal the absence of the film's protagonist – as well as the three activist friends he mourns. These scenes reinforce the sense of the film's inexorable movement forward into a future already decided but as yet unknown. The film has begun; there is no going back.

Consequently, a desire for Baldwin is highlighted even as it is shown to be impossible and misplaced. This is the very character of mourning, which is also the character of identity itself. But there is no going back to the source of the words heard in voiceover. Baldwin has died even before the film gets underway. His death is a condition of the film's existence. Nevertheless, through the technologies and poetics of literature and film, Baldwin's words linger and are carried along into the future, perhaps to review the sites of American antiblackness and white supremacy that persist in the director's and viewers' presents.

Considering theories of language, history, and meaning is productive as it helps explain *I Am Not Your Negro*'s production of a historically contingent (but not determinant) story about Baldwin and antiblackness through literary and cinematic archives. The story's coordinates – Baldwin's letter, his notes for "Remember This House," passages from *The Devil Finds Work*, as well as an FBI memorandum on Baldwin, print and film advertisements, archival photographs and film, and news footage – enable the film to navigate the echoes of Baldwin's wisdom in our present without insisting upon a final and foreseen destination. The film treats these coordinates as artifacts of an unfinished past-in-process, what Fred Moten names a "durational field rather than [an] event."[11] The project thereby participates in what Kara Keeling identifies, referencing historian Robin D.G. Kelley's book *Freedom Dreams: The Black Radical Imagination*, as "freedom dreams" – a liberationist poetics in which her own book, *Queer Times, Black Futures*, participates even as it "does not pretend to know where the insights it generates might lead."[12] Her endeavor seeks neither to make definitive sense out of nonsense nor to provide a closed reading of the archive, but "to remain aware of" possibilities for a future through a poetic commingling of extant materials that may be "felt and perceived even though – or especially if – it remains unrecognizable or unintelligible to current common sense."[13] Writing in terms that I maintain mirror those of *I Am Not Your Negro*, Keeling adds that "[w]e can think of what escapes these operations [of narrative and/or other formal devices of texts] as the content that exceeds its expression, though which poetry from the future might be perceived, yet not recognized."[14]

The poetics of Keeling's project describe the rich liberationist potentials of *I Am Not Your Negro*'s play with the archive, memory, and identification. It is significant that the film includes within it not only materials for "Remember This House" but also excerpts of Baldwin's published writings on film, which appear in Baldwin's book-length essay *The Devil Finds Work*. This inclusion stages a partnership of sorts between Peck and Baldwin in deconstructing the medium of film in order to identify and mobilize a cinematic vocabulary that can tell stories beyond the self-satisfying and implicitly (and explicitly) racist and homophobic nationalist stories (what Barthes calls "singular systems") of the Hollywood Golden Age.

Baldwin's essay is a curious text that shifts tenses unexpectedly and, even more oddly, tells the reader of things the author himself will never know or see. As a retrospective memoir, the essay explores both the limits of knowing and the limits of narration. Unlike the attempts at comprehensiveness explored by many conventional autobiographies, Baldwin's attempt fails – gloriously – to pierce the surface of the image. Instead, the essay takes seriously the misreadings and misunderstandings that would eventually come to constitute what Baldwin calls "all those hang-ups I didn't yet know I had."[15] It is these errors of memory and identification that *I Am Not Your Negro* takes up again to replay in the present.

There are canny slippages of characterization in Baldwin's writing, such as where he writes that he "knew about Booker T. Washington less than I knew about my father's mother, who had been born a slave, and who died in our house when I was a little."[16] Only the rules of English grammar maintain order in this passage, designating the fraternal grandmother (not Washington) as the formerly enslaved person who died in the Baldwins' house. Such confusions about origins suffuse Baldwin's essay, most especially where he writes of the important but somehow insignificant fact that the father to whom he refers in the first chapter is not his biological father – a fact he acknowledges in retrospect but with a commitment to narrating the truth of his childhood as he knew it, a childhood in which he believed his stepfather was indeed his biological father. Baldwin, writing about his childhood assessment of Dostoyevsky's *Crime and Punishment*, puts into language what can be understood as the phenomenological wonderment of learning through one's encounter with a work of representation: "I did not believe in any of these people so much as I believed in their situation, which I suspected, dreadfully, to have something to do with my own."[17] If there is a more succinct description of how the humanities work upon us, I would be eager to read it.

Baldwin, in other words, tells the truth as it is experienced and lived rather than as an historical event that must be corroborated and confirmed. His writing makes for generative material for the *I Am Not Your Negro* film project because it "exceeds its expression ... [and] also produces a surplus, one that cannot be seen or understood, but is nevertheless present as affect."[18] Baldwin does not give up on the mistakes and lies precisely because they are constitutive of his self. These very mistakes and lies, never fully processed or consumed by Baldwin's text, become in turn the material that the film will work over to work upon us in our own time. Never depleted nor consigned to an irretrievable past, the deceitful images of the Black subject and of the wider American romance with and against racism reemerge in Peck's film as clips and stills of classical and old Hollywood, carrying along with them the sentiments they have accrued from Baldwin's prior re-viewings.

Within a poetics that appreciates the unforeseen and unpredictable sense, meanings, and affects to come, re-viewings do not signal a loss or failing. In this instance, the principle that an historical document must be updated to respond seamlessly to a present (a kind of attempt at retroactive continuity in the documentary medium) is to be rejected in favor of the illuminating fissures of temporal displacement. To appreciate the re-viewing as art, one must therefore dispense with this investment in the "update" in order to acknowledge that something new is being brought into the world by drawing upon the past. Tellingly, Peck resists the appellation of adaptation – a term that suggests an updating that fully consumes its source material in order to produce something new and more applicable to the current moment. In describing his process, Peck writes of knowing at the early stages of the project that "[i]t could not be an adaptation, or a simple compilation, let alone a chronological narration."[19] Even in this rejection of overworking (adaptation) or underworking (compilation) or organizing (narrating) as a desirable process, Peck's aversion to "adaptation" might be understood best as a resistance to fixity and the illusion of unmediated representation that would presume to close the text, rendering the film, in Barthes's logic, "readerly" rather than "writerly," and one for whom the viewer "is left with no more than the poor freedom either to accept or reject the text."[20]

The film that results is not, it is true, a straightforward adaptation, one that conceals the influence and labor of the director in favor of an illusion of unmediated presentation. Instead, it is a worked-upon text that documents how Baldwin has worked upon Peck and how Peck attempts to convert that work into a sensible and communicable but ultimately unfinished object. It is evidence of a process of making sense that is singular and unavoidably subjective. The challenge of this film is to render the project of a process of comprehending itself comprehensible in cinematic terms.

The intermittent returns to the black screen, accruing white text, and soundtrack of keys clacking as the words are read anchor the film in the utterance of Baldwin's present even as the variety of footage – rolling landscapes of sky, of traffic, snips of film and still advertisements, movie excerpts, news footage, and, of course, interviews with the man himself – usefully trouble the temporal referents of Baldwin's words. An instance of such an interplay of meaning and time follows the montage of white male politicians apologizing for their various unnamed trespasses superimposed over a purple California sunset. The litany of apologies resolves with Baldwin's discussion of the misguided American virtue of immaturity, heard as a voiceover read by Jackson. The declaration retroactively classifies the preceding apologies as a symptom of this false virtue. However, Baldwin's words go on to link this condition to the figure of John Wayne – a shift that the film uses as an occasion to cut to stills of some of Wayne's cinematic appearances. The effect of this cut is to interrogate the prescience which we might attribute to Baldwin. But the film resists framing Baldwin as a fortune-teller, preferring instead to show him as a man commenting upon his own era. That the era and consequently Baldwin's words resound so pitch-perfectly in our present is instead made the point of the sequence.

Baldwin himself remarks upon the difficulty in creating a cinematic project that resists the discursive systems inclined toward closure. To be sure, Baldwin has nothing good to say about his own experience with Hollywood's attempts to translate his writing into a screenplay of *The Autobiography of Malcolm X*. But the indictment is not of translation, per se – after all, Baldwin admits he has hopes for the translation process – but of the master discourse to which his language is being submitted. The language is that of the Hollywood movie that can abide no ambiguity, no humanity to its Black characters, privileging what Baldwin calls "the 'action' line [which works primarily] in the interest of 'entertainment' values."[21] Parsing his critique, one detects a justified aversion to Hollywood's profit-driven view of entertainment – an understandable aversion for an author so fully committed to the representation of humanity's complexities. *I Am Not Your Negro* is not a Hollywood film, either by the standards of the industry (it was produced [which is to say funded] and distributed by non-US corporations and US independent houses, not Hollywood studios[22]) nor by the aesthetic precepts of plot (as Baldwin defines it) and entertainment in their privileging of action and resolution over art and poetry.

Indeed, the film *I Am Not Your Negro*, to the extent that it emerges from the specific unfinished project of Baldwin's own notes and letters toward "Remember This House," chronicles Baldwin's own strivings toward an identity and a vocabulary that could ethically and more or less accurately accommodate the positionality of a gay, middle-aged, African American, former expatriate, male-identified writer amidst the crisis of America's lethal struggles of the civil rights movement. The trinity of deaths – Medgar Evers, Malcolm X, and Martin Luther King, Jr. – seem to throw Baldwin into no mere emotional turmoil but into a true existential crisis about his being and his purpose in the world. One of the film's intertitles, displaying the word "Witness," underscores how Baldwin understood his journey during the civil rights era to be one of overcoming the role of mere spectator and "to accept … that part of my responsibility – as a witness – was to move as largely and as freely as possible, to write the story and to get it out."[23]

The gravity of Baldwin's notion of the witness can be located in one of the texts that informed his faith and vision of the world: the Christian bible and in particular the role of the two witnesses in the book of Revelations. On the cusp of a new era, the witnesses stand as "prophets who will eventually bring 'every people, tribe, language and nation' to the millennial age," even if the cost of this divine task is their own deaths.[24]

Baldwin's statement about witnessing is preceded in both the manuscript and the film (heard in voiceover) with a litany of identities that Baldwin claims he is not. Not "a Black Muslim" or "a Black Panther" or "a member of the NAACP" or even one who had "to deal with the criminal state of Mississippi" or "to sweat cold sweat after decisions involving hundreds of thousands of lives," Baldwin navigates these coordinates, marked by his friends and fellow African Americans, to arrive at his own identity – that of witness.[25] The identity he claims is, much like the identities he rejects, produced in relation to a context. He resolves to take up the task of viewing the movement "in passing," "to move as largely and freely as possible," and to write.[26]

This freedom of movement that rejects even as it acknowledges identity formations has the possibility of engendering liberation through bearing witness and taking note. Adapting Elizabeth Freeman's formulation of queer temporality to foreground the implications of queer spatiality as well, Keeling indicates "how queer spaces and indeed 'queerness' as a material practice call attention to the instability of existing relations, the (im)possibility of a rupture in any moment whatever," that might "proliferate unpredictable connections and encounters between seemingly random, exhausted, or useless things."[27]

Her highlighting of the radical potential of queer temporalities resonates with Moten's characterization of Black radical work in the break. Refusing identitarian closure in this passage, Baldwin sets himself up for a dynamic reconstruction of the self, one whose motive Moten describes as "the sexual differentiation of sexual difference."[28] With this appreciation of Black radical queer potentiality in mind, we might well see Baldwin's self-identification as a roaming, reporting witness to be a modality of queerness, one that bears in its resistance to fixity the potential to break open existing texts into new paradigms of liberation.

This interpretation of queerness might also have the effect of satisfying the film viewers' desire to see the queer Baldwin. While *I Am Not Your Negro* is not a biography and should not, therefore, be expected to account for Baldwin's (self-)identification as queer, his queerness may well usefully supply a fleeting logic to the film's structure of sensemaking. Baldwin appears to preview the film's fugitive engagement with its subject's sexuality where he declares, amidst a discussion of Stanley Kramer's 1968 film *The Defiant Ones* (which *I Am Not Your Negro* also screens), "I doubt that Americans will ever be able to face the fact the word, homosexual, is not a noun."[29] Baldwin goes on to add that "[t]he root of this word, as Americans use it ... simply involves a terror of any human touch, since any human touch can change you."[30] In other words, according to Baldwin, in an apparent prediction of Freeman's, Keeling's, and Moten's theories, queerness is change, the possibility of which subtends the conservative American terror of change that includes not only sexuality but also race.

A queered identity is presented as a resistance to stasis through the film's depictions of movement and contemplation. Halfway through the reading of the letter to Acton, the image cuts to a tracking shot of the elevated tracks in Baldwin's birthplace of Harlem, New York, as seen from below. Muted police sirens and a piano melody join the soundtrack as Jackson continues Baldwin's letter. A nearly unnoticeable dissolve halfway through the letter creates the illusion of continuous space and of moving forward toward a never-reached vanishing point before another dissolve focuses on the shadows cast on the ground by the tracks and proceeds, still, to follow them into an unknown distance, highlighting Baldwin's pronouncement of his "journey."

It does seem fair to interrogate whether the film's silence regarding Baldwin's sexuality renders the film project an exploitative one – a documentary that recruits Baldwin's image to tell its own story at the expense of the subject's actual views. This issue, however, is not one of authenticity. The writerly text, the text that only comes into being at the conjunction of the reader and the work (here, the work that constellates in the literary figure and biographical subject known as James Baldwin), can never be exactly inauthentic, though it can prove unproductive as an exercise and not useful for any but the reader-made-filmmaker.

Keeling's recent work on the queer Black subject in cinematic time helpfully addresses the consternation of Baldwin's largely absent sexuality in *I Am Not Your Negro*. Discussing the character M—— of the film *The Aggressives* (Daniel Peddle, 2005), Keeling validates this queer woman's escape from her military post and also of the film's narrative as a condition of Black queer life. "[B]y 'abruptly disappearing' and thereby refusing to become a conscript of war, M—might live ... [albeit living] unprotected and vulnerable."[31] Recognizing her own spectatorial and intellectual desires to know as structurally analogous to the designs of capture mobilized by the state, Keeling explodes the binary of out versus closeted into a far more meaningful and nuanced appreciation of narrative frustration and elusiveness:

> If disappearing enables M—to live, dragging M—into my sight here implicates my own work in the very processes and situations I seek to illuminate and challenge. ... The fact that M—must disappear from the film's narrative highlights the ways that a critical apparatus predicated upon making visible hidden images, sociocultural formations, ideas, concepts, and other things, always drags what interests it onto the terrain of power and the struggles through which that power is contested and/or (re)produced. On this terrain, the benefits of visibility are unevenly distributed.[32]

Keeling's caution against privileging the visible as the site of liberation returns us to the radical work of the break which can be usefully understood in cinematic terms as analogous to the cut. Indeed, Baldwin's discussion of the miscegenated queer potentiality of the farewell scene in Norman Jewison's 1967 film *In the Heat of the Night* (a scene staged provocatively at a train station – unconsciously, it would seem, linking movement to queerness) is reviewed in *I Am Not Your Negro*. The crosscuts that undergird the reaction shots between the Black and white man become, formally, the place where "the kissing will have to start" (Figures 1.1 and 1.2).[33]

Baldwin's contemplation of the forestalled queer interracial kiss between the characters portrayed by Sidney Poitier and Rod Steiger appears in his essay *The Devil Finds Work*. There, Baldwin expresses his "aware[ness] that men do not kiss each other in American films, nor, for the most part, in America, nor do the black detective and the white Sheriff kiss here."[34] The film *I Am Not Your Negro* elects to feature this

Figure 1.1 Sidney Poitier as Virgil Tibbs in *In the Heat of the Night* (Norman Jewison, 1967).

Figure 1.2 Rod Steiger as Sheriff Gillespie in *In the Heat of the Night* (Norman Jewison, 1967).

scene and declaration just after another of Baldwin's cinematic considerations: the interracial heterosexual kiss between Poitier and Katharine Houghton in *Guess Who's Coming to Dinner* (Stanley Kramer, 1967). Of this latter film, Baldwin writes, "*Guess Who's Coming to Dinner* may prove, in some bizarre way, to be a milestone, because it is really quite impossible to go any further in that particular direction. The next time, the kissing will have to start."[35] It is an odd declaration since the kissing has already started rather early in the film. When *I Am Not Your Negro* abuts this declaration and scenes of the film against Baldwin's comments on the absence (or, better, invisibility) of the queer kiss in *In the Heat of the Night* and its farewell scene, it invites a reassessment of the screen kiss as in line with the radical queer touch that Baldwin notes can produce change. The longing gazes and secretive smiles of Poitier and Steiger touch in the cut, which is both a cinematic poetic strategy and "the space between expression and meaning or between meaning and reference [that] remains an experience of meaning."[36]

Comprised of cuts and movements, *I Am Not Your Negro* offers a Black radical queer revision of Baldwin for the current moment. Rather than impose coherence in a style more common in historical documentaries relying heavily upon voiceover, the film lets the omissions and obfuscations of the archive retain their silence, compelling the film to contemplate its own desires and limitations. While there is certainly much to learn about the Baldwin presented in *I Am Not Your Negro*, the film, through its self-reflexive gestures, resists the certainty of knowing, preferring instead the contemplation that comes from encountering what cannot be known, what is left out, and what is artfully omitted. The cinematic gestures the film utilizes are disruptive and haunting as they return the viewer to the vocabulary, and in particular the movement, of the film. In so doing, they fulfill Baldwin's assertion that "[t]he language of the camera is the language of our dreams."[37]

Notes

1 Matt Brim explains that "[t]he queer Baldwin is not simply the liberatory or the visionary or the multiple Baldwin but rather the paradoxical Baldwin." Matt Brim, *James Baldwin and the Queer Imagination* (Ann Arbor: The University of Michigan Press, 2017), 2. Similarly, Cora Kaplan and Bill Schwarz critique the reductiveness of the formulation, stating that

> [f]or too long one Baldwin has been pitted against another Baldwin, producing a series of polarities that has skewed our understanding: his art against his politics; his fiction against his nonfiction; his early writings against his late writings; American Baldwin against European Baldwin; black Baldwin against queer Baldwin.

Cora Kaplan and Bill Schwarz, "Introduction: America and Beyond," in *James Baldwin: America and Beyond*, eds. Kaplan and Schwarz (Ann Arbor: The University of Michigan Press, 2011), 3.

2 My reference to cruising dystopia is a reference to José Muñoz's *Cruising Utopia: The Then and There of Queer Futurity* (New York: New York University Press, 2009) in which Muñoz, by way of Samuel Delany, identifies the utopian possibilities in forms of queer (male) sociality that

overcome and undermine the cordoned-off and closeted individuality of heteronormative societies.
3 Raoul Peck, "Introduction: On a Personal Note," in *I Am Not Your Negro: A Major Motion Picture Directed by Raoul Peck*, ed. Raoul Peck (New York: Vintage, 2017), ix.
4 Michel Foucault, "History, Discourse and Discontinuity," in *Foucault Live: (Interviews, 1961–1984)*, ed. Sylvère Lotringer, trans. Lysa Hochroth and John Johnston (New York: Semiotext(e), 1996), 42.
5 C.L.R. James, *The Black Jacobins: Toussaint l'Ouverture and the San Domingo Revolution* (New York: Vintage, 1989).
6 See Roland Barthes, *Mythologies*, trans. Annette Lavers (New York: Hill & Wang, 1972); Frantz Fanon, *Black Skin, White Masks*, trans. Richard Philcox (New York: Grove Press, 2008).
7 Roland Barthes, *S/Z: An Essay*, trans. Richard Miller (New York: Hill and Wang, 1974), 4.
8 Barthes, *S/Z*, 4.
9 Fred Moten, *In the Break: The Aesthetics of the Black Radical Tradition* (Minneapolis: University of Minnesota Press, 2003), 85.
10 James Baldwin, *Remember This House* (incomplete ms.); reprinted in *I Am Not Your Negro*, ed. Raoul Peck (New York: Vintage, 2017), 5.
11 Fred Moten, *Black and Blur* (Durham, NC and London: Duke University Press, 2017), xii. Moten makes this distinction in order to recognize, following Saidiya Hartman, that slavery is not an object of discrete historical investigation but an ongoing concept that inevitably also defines the terms of freedom as we know them "throughout the history of man." See Saidiya Hartman, *Scenes of Subjection: Terror, Slavery, and Self-Making in Nineteenth-Century America* (Oxford: Oxford University Press, 1997).
12 Kara Keeling, *Queer Times, Black Futures* (New York: New York University Press, 2019), xv.
13 Keeling, *Queer Times, Black Futures*, 83.
14 Keeling, *Queer Times, Black Futures*, 83.
15 James Baldwin, "The Devil Finds Work (1976)," in *Collected Essays: Notes of A Native Son / Nobody Knows My Name / The Fire Next Time / No Name in the Street / The Devil Finds Work*, ed. Toni Morrison (New York: The Library of America, 1998), 483.
16 Baldwin, "The Devil Finds Work," 485.
17 Baldwin, "The Devil Finds Work," 485.
18 Keeling, *Queer Times, Black Futures*, 82.
19 Peck, "Introduction," xvii.
20 Barthes, *S/Z*, 4.
21 Baldwin, "The Devil Finds Work," 553.
22 The production companies are Arte France, Independent Lens, Barthes, 4, Radio Télévision Suisse (RTS), Shelter Prod, and Velvet Film. The US distribution company is Magnolia Pictures.
23 James Baldwin, *Remember This House* (incomplete ms.); reprinted in Baldwin and Peck, *I Am Not Your Negro*, 31.
24 Lynne Joyrich, "American Dreams and Demons," *Black Scholar* 48, no. 1 (2018): 31. The witness at the end of days is mentioned in Revelation 11:3–12.

25 James Baldwin, *Remember This House* (incomplete ms.); reprinted in Baldwin and Peck, *I Am Not Your Negro*, 30–31.
26 Keeling, *Queer Times, Black Futures*, 87.
27 Keeling, *Queer Times, Black Futures*, 87.
28 Moten, *In the Break*, 85.
29 Baldwin, "The Devil Finds Work," 529.
30 Baldwin, "The Devil Finds Work," 529.
31 Keeling, *Queer Times, Black Futures*, 100.
32 Keeling, *Queer Times, Black Futures*, 100.
33 James Baldwin, "Sidney Poitier (1968)," in *The Cross of Redemption: Uncollected Writings*, ed. Randall Kenan (New York: Vintage, 2011), 227.
34 Baldwin, "The Devil Finds Work," 519.
35 Baldwin, "Sidney Poitier," 227.
36 Moten, *In the Break*, 92. One is also brought to think of Nathaniel Mackey's formulation of the "sexual cut," a principle of envisioning that also informs Moten's theory of the break. See Nathaniel Mackey, *Bedouin Hornbook* (Lexington: University of Kentucky, 1986).
37 Baldwin, "The Devil Finds Work," 504.

2 James Baldwin's embodied absence

I Am Not Your Negro and filmic corporeality

Laura Rascaroli

> Why, then, a body? Because only a body can be cut down or raised up, because only a body can touch or not touch. A spirit can do nothing of the sort. A "pure spirit" gives only a formal and empty index of a presence entirely closed in on itself. A body opens this presence; it presents it; it puts presence outside of itself; it moves presence away from itself, and, by that very fact, it brings others along with it.[1]

On 13 May 1975, artist Fabio Mauri's installation *Intellettuale* (*Intellectual*) took place on the steps outside the Modern Art Gallery of Bologna on the occasion of its inauguration. Poet, writer, and director Pier Paolo Pasolini sat on a chair in front of the audience, clad in a white shirt, while his film *The Gospel According to St. Matthew* (*Il Vangelo secondo Matteo*, 1964) was projected onto his torso. The photographs of Mauri's installation by Antonio Masotti show Pasolini's darkened silhouette, the bright images of the film turning his chest into an incarnate screen (Figure 2.1).

As Giacinto Di Pietrantonio has written of the installation,

> The art of Mauri who, like Pasolini's, has a religious weight beyond the dogma, shows Pasolini's sacred body in the dark, mystically lit only by the light of the projection, a "radiograph of the spirit" of the poet's body which, shortly thereafter, will be sacrificed on the beach of Ostia, ending the life of the dissenting intellectual, radically active in condemning state powers. For Mauri, the artist is an intellectual in the Benjaminian sense, for he is not the one who appears romantically alone and lost in the face of the power of the world, but he who has responsibilities towards the world itself and participates in the world.[2]

Figure 2.1 Incarnate screen: *The Gospel According to St. Matthew* (*Il Vangelo secondo Matteo*, 1964) projected onto the torso of its director, Pier Paolo Pasolini, during the performance *Intellettuale* (Fabio Mauri, 13 May 1975). Photo: Antonio Masotti/Cineteca di Bologna.

Although the idea of a radiograph of the artist's spirit is evocative, the photographs, I would argue, are more strongly suggestive of the corporeality of Pasolini's cinema, and of its inscription onto the authorial body, which bears his film like a cross. *The Gospel According to St. Matthew* has often been seen in light of its autobiographical overtones, including Pasolini's desire to have Christ played by a famous poet as a sort of stand-in for himself (Yevgeny Yevtushenko and Jack

Kerouac were both considered), and the casting of his mother Susanna as the older Virgin Mary.[3] Pasolini, furthermore, notoriously characterized himself in a Christ-like manner in some of his work, especially the poem "La crocifissione" ("The Crucifixion").[4] In spite of declaring himself not a Catholic, he identified with Jesus as the ideal embodiment of a "scandalous" mode of existence, characterized by protest and resistance to power. Pasolini's controversial figure was at once an object of fascination and of abhorrence for his contemporaries. John Di Stefano has noted that "[c]aught somewhere between revulsion and fascination, Italians developed an obsession with Pasolini's body," at a time when the queer body was vehemently repressed and reviled in Italian society.[5] Pasolini's strategy in his oeuvre, and beyond it, responded to his choice of making recourse "to the essential signifier of an 'authentic' body as a public locus of discourse, in response to the exclusion from discourse and from narrative sexual ideologies."[6]

I have evoked Pasolini's foregrounding of himself both as a "public locus of discourse" and as the embodied screen in Fabio Mauri's *Intellettuale* to begin to flesh out the "filmic body" of Raoul Peck's *I Am Not Your Negro* (2016). James Baldwin's deliberate deployment of his own body as an arena for debate beyond his oeuvre, that is, in his lectures and interviews and on televised debates, bears more than a similarity with Pasolini's textual and extratextual strategies – and is also central to Peck's film and its argument. My interest here lies in understanding *I Am Not Your Negro* as an essay – as a work that articulates its argument filmically, rather than exclusively through verbal intelligence – and in showing how this filmic argument, which is inherently political, arises gradually from a complex corporeal discourse. *I Am Not Your Negro*, indeed, deals extensively with the body and images of bodies. These include the bodies of the three heroes/martyrs of the civil rights movement – Medgar Evers, Malcolm X, and Martin Luther King, Jr. – all killed in the course of five years, from 1963 to 1968; those of slaves, who are pictured in archival images while working, entertaining, suffering, dying, decomposing; and those – defiant and terrified, rebellious and brutalized – of demonstrators and victims of civilian and police racial violence in the US, both in the past and today. More relevantly to my point, *I Am Not Your Negro*'s argument is built on the plurality of the body: the body as physical substance and as imaginary projection, as intimate reality and as social construct, as materiality and as metaphor. "Which body? We have several," epigrammatically asked Roland Barthes in his autobiography.[7] For both Baldwin and Pasolini, then, the discourse of identity is an embodied and autobiographical political discourse. Gesturing already from its title to an autobiographical field, to a denied identity, and to a scandalous body politics, *I Am Not Your Negro* draws on Baldwin's textual discourse on the body and extratextual deployment of his own body, but it also uses filmic means to transform his body into cinematic argument – into a screen onto which a racialized projection is invited from the audience. This transformation takes place in the very last sequence, but it builds on a complex strategy that unfolds throughout the film.

In 1979, James Baldwin wrote a letter to his agent Jay Acton describing his plans for a book which would recount the lives and deaths of his friends Medgar Evers, Malcolm X, and Martin Luther King, Jr. Peck's documentary takes its lead from this letter and from Baldwin's unfinished essay/memoir, *Remember This House*, a book that he found it impossible to write, and of which he completed only 30 pages before his death in 1987. It also draws passages from Baldwin's memoir *No Name in the Street* (1972) and from *The Devil Finds Work* (1976), his brilliant critique of Hollywood cinema. All of these adapted essayistic passages, voiced by Samuel L. Jackson, are intertwined with footage of Baldwin himself, lecturing or participating in televised debates. The eloquent, lucid, charismatic speech of James Baldwin, thus, subtends and supports the entire film. *I Am Not Your Negro*, however, speaks with its own essayistic voice too.

I Am Not Your Negro's argument is characterized by an epic scope, which can be summarized through Baldwin's statement, spoken in the film by Jackson, that "The story of the Negro in America is the story of America. It is not a pretty story." In other words, Peck's film takes on and corroborates Baldwin's contention that the history of Blacks is not part of American history; it *is* American history. By disconnecting the two, or by subordinating one to the other, in dominant historical narratives, what is lost is a deeper understanding of America as a country, of its roots, its culture, its politics – and of its present too. The film, accordingly, sets out to show how, in North American history, the "Negro" body is marked by the invisibility to which the white society condemned it: it is concealed and negated, at once as a human body, as a suffering body, and as a sexual body. At the same time, it is the site of an almost archetypal fantasy that, Baldwin argues, is essential to the construct of whiteness: that of the "Nigger." The mental image of the "Nigger" for Baldwin gives rise to certain other images that neutralize it, such as the innocuous, submissive "Negro," as well as to an overwhelming number of media-fabricated images that present the US and the American dream as inherently white. Through extensive use of archival material illustrating and supporting the voiceover's critique, *I Am Not Your Negro* shows how, over the decades, an endless series of images from television, film, and advertising – many of which relied on the boldness of Technicolor – cancelled out the reality of Black America. An ample range of cultural and commercial products is covered by the film to demonstrate and illustrate Baldwin's points. The history of Hollywood is represented, from early film to classical westerns, from musicals to Doris Day films. Characters of color are shown to have been either entirely absent from the screen or reduced to vicious enemies to be eradicated (like the Native Americans in classical westerns), lazy types, or one-dimensional servants and entertainers. Baldwin's critique of later films with Black main characters and stars such as Sidney Poitier, including *The Defiant Ones* (Stanley Kramer, 1957), *In the Heat of the Night* (Norman Jewison, 1967), and *Guess Who's Coming to Dinner* (Stanley Kramer, 1967), shows that "[a]lthough these films were widely praised for their supposedly liberal racial politics at the time of their release, […] they further entrenched unequal relations between blacks and whites."[8] As Baldwin argued in his writings, these films ultimately were about reassuring white spectators about their own innocence and ensuring they could preserve their self-image.

To a great extent, then, the film's argument coincides with Baldwin's argument, as unfolded through his work and interviews, and its essayistic logic and eloquent force are those of Baldwin's prose and speech. However, *I Am Not Your Negro* does more than simply reproduce Baldwin's words and illustrate them. If the Black body is obliterated, erased, and absent from the image of American society, then it follows that a Black body needs to be summoned, reconstructed, and reincarnated, precisely in order to reveal its lack. *I Am Not Your Negro* aims to do so via a number of strategies. At a most immediate level, the film presents us with an abundance of images of Black bodies to contrast their absence from white-dominated media and public discourse. These images include those of Baldwin's friends Medgar Evers, Malcolm X, Martin Luther King, Jr., and Lorraine Hansberry, and of their friends and families. Through the lens of Baldwin's address to his agent and his reader, these people are conjured beyond their historical significance or iconic status; they are represented in flesh and bones, so to speak, in their humanity, their character, their lives and relations, and their physical features (the tone of their voice, how they stood, how they laughed, how they pronounced a specific word), and not just as historical symbols of a political and civil struggle. Lesser known figures too are brought into focus: those who stood up for their rights, demonstrated in the streets, on buses, on their way to school, and just dared to exist. The film also presents us with many images of violated bodies – enslaved, threatened, humiliated, wounded, and murdered. Among them are the images of the corpses of Evers, Malcolm X, and Martin Luther King, Jr., and of their funerals and their mourners, but also descriptions of where and how Baldwin learned about their deaths, and the resulting physical anguish he experienced. Peck also goes beyond Baldwin's life span and summons for us more recent images of violence, which we have witnessed on television since the early 1990s, and now through our mobile media – from Rodney King's videotaped beating to more recent police brutality captured by citizens' mobile phone cameras and widely shared via the Black Lives Matter campaign. This move of the film bolsters Baldwin's long view of "the story of the Negro in America" in its historical significance and connects the bodies of recent victims to those of the earlier civil rights and Black Power movements, all the way back to those of slaves working and dying in cotton plantations. In so doing, the film historicizes contemporary events, by placing them in a continuum; equally, it actualizes historical events, by showing that the past is not past – to paraphrase William Faulkner.[9]

Through archival images and Baldwin's own commentary, therefore, we are exposed to the reality of Black lived experience in American history, through to our day. The ideological nature of images of "the Negro" that dominated the media since the origin of the cinema is exposed and decried. One point at which this becomes eminently tangible through filmic form, rather than verbal commentary, is the sudden transition from a glittering romantic sequence in the Doris Day film *Lover Come Back* (1961) to graphic photographs of lynched bodies. The visual shock produced by the jump cut exposes the extraordinary violence concealed in the alluring obfuscation of the Hollywood dream and is remindful of some of the most radical montages and superimpositions in *Histoire(s) du cinéma* (1989–1999), Jean-Luc Godard's video essay on a century of imbrication of cinema and history.

While *I Am Not Your Negro*'s most evident strategy as regards its discourse on corporeality is that of embracing and illustrating Baldwin's own argument on the effacement of real Black bodies and their ideological obfuscation, Peck also goes beyond it, by working with and via James Baldwin's own body in the film. Here too, to an extent, the film straightforwardly echoes Baldwin's strategies – but also takes them further. Baldwin's real body, as already discussed, is present in the film through still photography and footage of his lectures and his participation in televised interviews and debates. The latter best reveal Baldwin's corporeal strategy, where his own body becomes a provocative instrument of signification and of denunciation. The centrality of embodiment to Baldwin's thought is evident when reading his oeuvre and is perfectly encapsulated by the following statement of his: "Within the body of the Negro press all the wars and falsehoods, all the decay and dislocation and struggle of our society are seen in relief."[10] The body, then, is right at the center of Baldwin's historical critique, and of his essayistic design too. Baldwin's core aim in his essay work, which the film brings into relief, is to summon the effaced and mystified body of the "Negro." In the excerpts of televised interviews included in the film, Baldwin uses his own body to do just that. Sitting in the television studio, he holds himself as irrefutable material presence. On the one hand, his body – singular, connoted, self-possessed – is a "body of evidence"; it testifies to the existence of real men and women, who have been removed from the public eye. On the other hand, it is a resolute, resisting body, which stubbornly refuses to reflect back the reassuring persona of "the Negro" (intended as the innocuous, submissive "Uncle Tom" figure that was depicted as happy with his place in white America), in spite of the significant advances that "the Negro" has made in American society, as interviewers point out to him, quite overtly reproaching him for his "unhappiness" and anger. Baldwin's stance in these interviews is to present a body of resistance, and to shatter misconceptions, reflecting his thought that

> the Negro has never been as docile as white Americans wanted to believe. That was a myth. We were not singing and dancing down on the levee – we were trying to keep alive; we were trying to survive. It was a very brutal system. The Negro has never been happy in his place.[11]

The film's key achievement, however, is to evoke (without completely actualizing) the fullness of Baldwin's body. This happens through filmic means, by the introduction of a voiceover. It is the voiceover that, with its own "body," takes the fragmented image of Baldwin and gives it flesh. Such flesh is, of course, filmic; yet, not only does this not detract from its impact on the film's argument, but it is its force. As a documentary, *I Am Not Your Negro* carries out a historical/biographical work of testimony and assemblage, and is a vehicle for Baldwin's ideas; as an essay, it suggests a corporeal fullness to Baldwin's textual fragments by giving them a filmic voice. This fullness is the site of a productive ambiguity that demands exegesis.

Baldwin's voice is indeed present in the film, audible in the footage of his public performances. But the film adds a second voice, performed by Samuel L. Jackson. It is significant that at least one critic deemed that Jackson here "gives his best performance in more than a decade."[12] Comments such as this reflect the importance of the voiceover in the film, which has been credited with giving "fresh voice" to Baldwin.[13] For another critic, the voiceover makes of Baldwin a "quiet, meditative presence" throughout the film.[14] But the voiceover, I argue, is not just there to make Baldwin present, "fresh," or current. While the film's voiced contents come directly from Baldwin's essayistic writings (in which, incidentally, he most frequently adopted a first-person narrator), the voice itself also signifies. Voice's autonomy from signification, argued by theorists including Julia Kristeva and Roland Barthes, makes space for the purely sonorous, for the bodily element of the vocal utterance, for the Barthesian "grain" of the voice.[15] This grain testifies to a displacement. If the filmed excerpts included in *I Am Not Your Negro* give us glimpses of Baldwin's public persona (and of his voice), the voiceover narration, with its personal address, intimate tone, and confessional attitude, suggests human fullness and embodied subjectivity; it evokes the man, and the essayist at the same time. The voice of Jackson's voiceover, however – and this is crucial – gestures to an embodiment by its absence. In a short text published in the book that accompanied the release of the film, editor Alexandra Strauss, referring to her work on the film and the role of the voiceover in the edit, remarks precisely on this absence, and on the impossibility of resurrecting Baldwin, when she asks,

> How do we connect a narrating voice that obviously could not be Baldwin's with the real footage of him speaking so eloquently? How could we achieve a discursive continuity between these two elements?[16]

Strauss leaves her question hanging, because the answer is that continuity is not achievable. In Barthesian terms, the grain "is the body in the voice as it sings, the hand as it writes, the limb as it performs."[17] And it is the grain that provides us with "the image of the body (the figure)."[18] The highly distinctive, performed, "raspy, hushed"[19] grain of Jackson's voiceover gives us a figure; it is iconogenic,[20] to use Michel Chion's term, for it impels us to figure an embodiment; it mediates a bodily image. As such, it is at once an index of presence (for we always perceive a voice as emanating from vocal organs, even when we do not see a body), and of misalignment and lack – those of the body of Baldwin, whose materiality is here mediated at once by discourse and by the grain of another man's voice. The voiceover, as a distinctly filmic device, is a body as it voice-performs, but here it also conjures up, and points at, the missing body of James Baldwin. Its ontological status is, therefore, profoundly ambiguous. It is an allusion and a displacement, and its ambiguity is further compounded by its difference from, and similarity with, James Baldwin's actual voice, which is also audible in the film. Jackson's voiceover, in this sense, is more than a narrative stratagem to convey Baldwin's thought, or a way to make him "fresh." If, on the one hand, it makes him more present, on the other hand, it makes a figure of him, in Barthes' sense: filmic flesh. And, in so doing, it creates the conditions for the film's most powerful argument, which is so central to the film to be encapsulated in its title.

This argument comes to fruition in between two bodies. As an actual, historicized body, Baldwin's appearance in the televised debates denounces the lack of true-to-life images of Black people on television and other screens. As filmic flesh – a figure in the film, at once present and absent, image and *acousmêtre* – he becomes the *possibility* of an embodiment. This possibility, this sheer potentiality allows it to expose the psychological processes of projection, which in film are often quite literal, and according to which the ego "projects" an id impulse out of a person and onto an other (here, a racialized other). This is nowhere more powerful than in the last sequence, in which Baldwin holds himself firmly before the camera and directly addresses his white television audience:

> What white people have to do is try to find out in their hearts why it was necessary for them to have a nigger in the first place. Because I am not a nigger. I'm a man. If I'm not the nigger here, and if you invented him, you the white people invented him, then you have to find out why. And the future of the country depends on that. Whether or not it is able to ask that question.

Shot in close-up, the sequence is nonfictional, but it could just as easily be fiction, given the radical, Godardian flatness of the image, further compounded by the abstraction of the black background and the central fixity of the camera, the swirls of cigarette smoke metafilmically revealing the gap between the lens and the profilmic (Figure 2.2).

Coming right at the end of the film, it draws on all our accumulated knowledge of Baldwin's body, on all its forms and meanings. Oscillating between image and materiality, figure and man, and exploiting the power of the screen as a compelling site of identification, Baldwin looks straight into the lens. Occupying the whole of the screen, and in fact coinciding with it, he invokes a phantasmatic projection, which cannot but flash in the (white) spectator's mind. In so doing, he holds up a mirror to his white audience, challenging it to confront its fantasy of the loathsome "Nigger" and to recognize its own moral corruption.

Figure 2.2 James Baldwin invokes a phantasmatic racialized projection onto his body during a televised debate. *I Am Not Your Negro* (Raoul Peck, 2016).

Baldwin's body at the end of *I Am Not Your Negro*, therefore, becomes a screen that provocatively invites a racialized projection onto itself, so as to reveal and reflect back the corrupt soul of white America. His body here is all at once material (the poised body sitting in the television studio), televised (for how the television camera frames it, frontally singling it out against the black backdrop and bringing it to the sitting rooms of countless Americans), and filmic (for how the film progressively constructs a discourse on corporeality that leads to this final moment). Similarly, Pier Paolo Pasolini's scandalous material and performing body in the installation *Intellettuale* turned into a screen that bore his own film like a cross – and not any film but a rendition of the *Gospel*. In a photograph of the performance taken from behind Pasolini's back, which reverses the perspective, Pasolini looks literally transfixed by the ray of light coming from the projector, as a Christological sacrificial victim. His queer body, in *Intellettuale* as in some of his own work, is thus the site of a scandalous identification with Christ.

In both Pasolini's and Baldwin's deployment of a corporeal identification, then, we can say that the author's body deliberately lends itself to become a "public locus of discourse," to use again Gordon's phrase on Pasolini's textual and, crucially for my argument, extratextual strategies. Both Pasolini and Baldwin chose to incarnate their intellectual production, which is thus quite literally made flesh. Albeit distinctly, both used their bodies as the site of a scandalous identification/projection to bring to light unspoken moral and ideological evils in mainstream white/patriarchal/heternormative society. Several reviewers, however, have noted how Baldwin's queerness is mostly silenced in Peck's film, possibly in the name of a more efficient focus on his blackness and on the civil rights movement, thus creating only a partial image of his embodiment, and its relevance in and for his oeuvre. This is problematic since, as Michael L. Cobb has remarked, "[q]ueerness and blackness are closely aligned in Baldwin's eyes – and with that connection he upset traditional, religious history about blackness by founding the race through queer sexuality."[21] Yet, aside from the mention of a 1966 FBI memorandum commenting that Baldwin "may be a homosexual and he appeared as if he may be one," the film does not delve into the racial politics of his sexuality:

> The apparent desire to represent Baldwin as the quintessential Race Man – a public spokesman and leader of African Americans with ostensibly straight bonafides – goes against not only the principles of Baldwin's work, but also the reality of his fraught position in the civil-rights movement as a queer black man. [...] viewers wouldn't know from the film's narrative slant how the experience of race and sexuality were closely intertwined for Baldwin.[22]

In a piece on "Queering *I Am Not Your Negro*," Robert J. Corber sets off from young Baldwin's queer identification with movie stars such as Bette Davis and Sylvia Sidney to analyze his complex relationship with his gayness in his writing. Corber shows how, for many critics of the time, Baldwin's homosexuality undermined his credentials as a spokesperson for the civil rights movement. He cites a telling 1963 article published in *Time*, which described him as a "nervous, slight, almost fragile figure, filled with frets and fears," implying he was "not, by any stretch of the imagination, a Negro leader."[23] It is known that Baldwin started to give credit to the line that equated militancy and masculinity, and, notoriously, he came close to endorsing homophobic views of homosexuality "as a white man's disease that robbed black men of their manhood."[24] Nevertheless, with reference to an interview by Baldwin with Richard Goldstein, Corber also shows that Baldwin's prose style "signified a repudiation of the dominant form of masculinity."[25] The passage is worth citing in full, because of its relevance for my argument on embodiment and projection:

> Baldwin suggested that men had invented the category of the faggot to protect themselves from the waywardness of their own desires.

Because of the norms governing masculinity, men could never express or act on their homoerotic impulses without undermining their claims to manhood; therefore they projected their sexual fantasies onto other men. Baldwin remarked that the figure of the faggot allowed men "to act out a sexual fantasy on the body of another man and not take any responsibility for it", and he exhorted the homosexual to recognize "that he is a sexual target for other men, and that is why he is despised, and why he is called a faggot."[26]

Hence, Baldwin's lending of his body to the phantasmatic racial projection of the "Nigger" figure cannot be separated from the homophobic projection of the "faggot."

If Pasolini's foregrounding of his queer body in *Intellettuale* and elsewhere was narcissistically overlaid by a scandalous discourse of Christological sacrifice, however, Baldwin's stance in the sequence of *I Am Not Your Negro* that I singled out is not sacrificial. Instead, Baldwin's body gives itself to a range of possibilities, which exist all at once, and as alternatives: the historical, individualized, queer Black body; an ideological absence and a representational void; the resisting "Negro" body; and even the loathsome, repellent "Nigger." In so doing, Baldwin's image evokes a great many cultural and ideological tropes, while stubbornly resisting cultural appropriation, stereotyping, and victimization. Within the overall design of the film, then, this move counteracts any temptation to articulate resistance merely as an "injury discourse" and any impulse "to render historical events through metaphors about the body, preferably a body that is wounded."[27] While *I Am Not Your Negro* is punctuated with wounded Black bodies, in his work, as reflected in the film too, Baldwin "vehemently opposes the recalcitrant acceptance of 'the divine right of suffering'."[28] Although a figure, and indeed because it is a figure, Baldwin's body in *I Am Not Your Negro* is not a metaphor – as clearly indicated by the long series of frontal portraits of "real" Black people from both the past and the present looking deliberately into the camera lens, interpellating the spectator. Their images are presented just before the described closing sequence of the film, in which Baldwin also looks into the lens and offers his body as an incarnate screen. As a result, they appear to be summoned by Baldwin's body and to repeat its gesture. To use Jean-Luc Nancy's words on Christ's resurrection and revelation, from the epigraph of this chapter: "Why then a body? Because only a body [...] puts presence outside of itself; [...] and, by that very fact, it brings others along with it."[29] Not a spirit but a body of flesh only can reveal a presence. Oscillating between figure and man, Baldwin's filmic body in *I Am Not Your Negro* puts presence outside of itself, bringing the missing Black body along with it.

Notes

1. Jean-Luc Nancy, *Noli Me Tangere: On the Raising of the Body*, trans. Sarah Clift, Pascale-Anne Brault and Michael Naas (New York: Fordham University Press, 2008), 48.
2. Giacinto Di Pietrantonio, "Fabio Mauri: No era nuevo," Fundación PROA Buenos Aires (2014), http://proa.org/esp/exhibition-fabio-mauri.php. My trans.
3. Pier Paolo Pasolini and Oswald Stack, *Pasolini on Pasolini: Interviews with Oswald Stack* (London: Thames and Hudson, 1969), 78.
4. Pier Paolo Pasolini, "La crocifissione" (1948–1949), in *Tutte le poesie*, ed. Walter Siti, vol. 1 (Milan: Mondadori, 2003), 467–468.
5. John Di Stefano, "Picturing Pasolini: Notes from a Filmmaker's Scrapbook," *Art Journal* 56, no. 2 (1997): 20.
6. Robert Gordon, *Pasolini: Forms of Subjectivity* (Oxford: Clarendon Press, 1996), 2–3.
7. Roland Barthes, *Roland Barthes by Roland Barthes*, trans. Richard Howard (London: Macmillan, 1977), 60.
8. Robert J. Corber, "Queering *I Am Not Your Negro*: Or Why We Need James Baldwin More than Ever," *James Baldwin Review* 3, no. 1 (2017): 162.
9. William Faulkner, *Requiem for a Nun* (New York: Vintage, 2011), 85.
10. James Baldwin, "The Harlem Ghetto" (1948), in *Notes of a Native Son* (Boston, MA: Beacon Press, 1984), 62–63.
11. James Baldwin, *Conversations with James Baldwin*, eds. Fred L. Stanley and Louis H. Pratt (Jackson: University Press of Mississippi, 1989), 42.
12. Violet Lucca, "*I Am Not Your Negro* Review: Race, Rage and the American Dream," *Sight and Sound* 27, no. 5 (May 2017), www.bfi.org.uk/news-opinion/sight-sound-magazine/reviews-recommendations/i-am-not-your-negro-raoul-peck-race-rage-american-dream.
13. Christopher John Farley, "*I Am Not Your Negro* Gives Fresh Voice to James Baldwin," *Wall Street Journal*, 25 January 2017.
14. Eric Kohn, "*I Am Not Your Negro* Review: Samuel L. Jackson Brings James Baldwin to Life in the Year's Most Important Oscar Nominee," *IndieWire*, 2 February 2017, www.indiewire.com/2017/02/i-am-not-your-negro-review-james-baldwin-raoul-peck-oscar-1201777014/.
15. Julia Kristeva, *Revolution in Poetic Language*, trans. Margaret Waller (New York: Columbia University Press, 1985); Roland Barthes, "The Grain of the Voice," in *Image, Music, Text*, trans. Stephen Heath (New York: Hill and Wang, 1977), 179–189.
16. Alexandra Strauss, "Editing *I Am Not Your Negro*," in *I Am Not Your Negro*, ed. Raoul Peck (London: Penguin, 2017), xx.
17. Barthes, "Grain," 188.
18. Barthes, "Grain," 189.
19. Lucca, "*I Am Not*."
20. Michel Chion, *Audio-Vision: Sound on Screen* (New York: Columbia University Press, 2019), 236.
21. Michael L. Cobb, "Pulpitic Publicity: James Baldwin and the Queer Uses of Religious Words," *GLQ: A Journal of Lesbian and Gay Studies* 7, no. 2 (2001): 300.

22 Dagmawi Woubshet, "The Imperfect Power of *I Am Not Your Negro*," *The Atlantic*, 8 February 2017, www.theatlantic.com/entertainment/archive/2017/02/i-am-not-your-negro-review/515976/.
23 Corber, "Queering," 166.
24 Corber, "Queering," 166.
25 Corber, "Queering," 168.
26 Corber, "Queering," 168.
27 Cobb, "Pulpitic Publicity," 288.
28 Douglas Field, "Pentecostalism and All That Jazz: Tracing James Baldwin's Religion," *Literature and Theology* 22, no. 4 (2008): 444.
29 Nancy, *Noli Me Tangere*, 48.

3 "Some One of Us Should Have Been There with Her"

Gender, race, and sexuality in *I Am Not Your Negro* and contemporary Black experimental documentary

Ellen C. Scott

> For, if they take you in the morning, they will be coming for us that night.
> —James Baldwin, Letter to Angela Davis, November 19, 1970.[1]

Sandra Bland. Ramarley Graham. Walter Scott. Michael Brown. Eric Garner. Freddie Gray. Tamir Rice. Philando Castile. Laquan McDonald. Renisha McBride. Oscar Grant. Anthony Lamar Smith.

The human response to this list turned anthem should be "Never forget" and "Never again." But the US justice system has given us an absurd and enraging stream of non-trials or non-indictments for the white officers who have murdered these unarmed citizens. This history of neglect, passivity, acceptance, and even applause in the face of the public murder of Black men is what is most centrally and acerbically revealed in Raoul Peck's *I Am Not Your Negro*, a film based on the words of James Baldwin, especially his unpublished work, *Remember This House*. However, the more indirect logic of the destruction of Black women remains firmly at the margins.

Peck's film innovates in challenging documentary's show-and-tell logic. Like Edward Bland in *The Cry of Jazz* (1959) and Yance Ford in *Strong Island* (2017), Peck experiments with the relationship between documentary, personal narrative, and fiction, and loosens the relationship between the sound and the image track. By linking Baldwin's words to images, both historical and contemporary, Peck makes room for a personal observational style – or even a kind of unconscious – to usurp documentary's conventional narrative order. For instance, Peck pairs Baldwin's words about the moral emptiness of American prosperity with a Technicolor sequence of pristine, fanciful, white picnic-goers in the musical *The Pajama Game* (George Abbott and Stanley Donen,

1957). This reappropriation of Hollywood's "decent" pleasures follows the logic of Baldwin's critical readings of American film images in *The Devil Finds Work*. Through appropriation, Peck uses film, the medium historically most responsible for spinning the white fantasy of disconnection from Black people, as an avenue to critique that very fantasy.

Widening the associative index, Peck pairs Baldwin's words with images not specifically referenced in them, moving beyond literal associations to a more abstract, elliptical set of connections stemming, seemingly, from an American unconscious. Through fabricated images of the surface of Mars, scratched archival home movies of Black boys in bunny suits, and pristine, canted 1950s color footage of white women in white outfits running against a cloudless blue sky, he ponderously reveals an underlying layer of possible meanings for Baldwin's words that cut to the deep of America's racist soul.

Peck's film reminds us of the moral mind of James Baldwin. He was calling white America to account for the obscenity of its racism and its effacement of the role of its purity and innocence complex in its project of colonial world domination. Peck achieves a curatorial feat in his selection and pairing of images and Baldwin's words. The juxtaposition of historical images (for example, Doris Day with Black lynching victims), the interposition of contemporary images and voices (from Ferguson protesters to Donald Trump), and the unhurried pace with which the film treads among Americana's image-bound lies sharpen its statement about American racism's ironies. For example, both the contemporary images of the South's swamps and willow trees which almost certainly bore strange fruit and the sudden, vibrant colorization of 1960s footage are part of the film's aesthetic historiography designed to point up the similarities between the 1960s and today.

I Am Not Your Negro is strongest in its acidic, urgent commentary on America's denial pathology. This commentary has lost none of its power since the 1970s, just as America has lost none of its white supremacy. As Richard Wright puts it, and Peck and Baldwin reveal, "The Negro problem in the United States has been and is a white problem. Whites created it and maintain it."[2] Baldwin's words not only make whiteness visible but demonstrate its peculiarity, its obsessions, and its perversities. Baldwin does this not jeeringly but to show that white absurdities define America. In tandem, Peck's images bring the inane violence of white "civilization" into poetic relief.

James Baldwin was a national treasure. Against the tide of white intellectual bombast, he spit truth that still sizzles, as we see on Peck's screen. It corrodes the American fantasy about a self-proclaimed innocence, which has compromised its moral soul and made room for unthinkable neglect. Peck bases his film on Baldwin's writings about the deaths of Medgar Evers, Malcolm X, and Martin Luther King, Jr. Laudably, Peck refuses to reduce the film to the story of a single heroic man, whether Baldwin, Malcolm, Medgar, or Martin, eschewing the documentary genre's paean modality that mystifies as it uplifts the memories of Black leaders. Instead, Peck looks at how these men, with all their differences, are collapsed into the target-bearing mold of the Black male figure.

But Baldwin's project is, like all intellectual endeavors, limited. Rather than examining or surmounting these limitations, Peck risks amplifying them. The film's construction of "the Negro," like that of Baldwin and Franz Fanon, is essentially and by default male. The anachronism of this construction is something that Peck does not probe or question. This is most tangible in Peck's half-hearted inclusion of Lorraine Hansberry, who, dead at 34, was arguably victim of just the kind of everyday racism that Black women experience and that is so often ignored. Did Peck marginalize Hansberry because unlike Martin, Malcolm, and Medgar, she was not assassinated? Sandra Bland. Lorraine Hansberry. Ella Baker. Eslanda Robeson. Henrietta Lacks. Was there not, in these women's lives, rebellion, and undoing, a pattern distinct from that of Malcolm, Martin, and Medgar, but also distinctly "Negro"?

Hansberry reminds us of the gendered nature of the racializing project and the specific kinds of deadly negligence – an often intimate, close-range, private neglect – that Black women have historically experienced. As Baldwin wrote after Hansberry's death, Lorraine – who had tried to convince Bobby Kennedy "that if the American state could not protect the lives of black citizens, then, presently, the entire State would find itself engulfed" – never lived "to see with the outward eye what she saw so clearly with the inward one." Baldwin insisted, "it is not at all far-fetched to suspect that what she saw contributed to the strain which killed her, for the effort to which Lorraine was dedicated is more than enough to kill a man."[3] While it may be said that speaking of Lorraine alongside Malcolm, Martin, and Medgar was not Baldwin's project, it behooves Peck, the contemporary interpreter, to ask, "why not?" That Peck departs from *Remember This House* and updates Baldwin's vision in other ways, suturing Baldwin's words to images of Ferguson protestors, makes his gender vacuum more puzzling. Gender critique is not expendable. The project of building "a politics that will change our lives and inevitably end our oppression," in the words of the Combahee River Collective, requires understanding the systematic entwining of race, class, gender, sexuality, and power.[4] Indeed, "if they take you in the morning" through the door of racialization, "they will be coming for us that night" through the door of misogyny. And we must not forget that Black women really were silenced within Black freedom struggles of the 1960s and beyond.⁵

There are a few scattered images of Black women in the film other than Hansberry. Peck dedicates a sequence to Baldwin's experience of seeing on a Paris newsstand the photo of 15-year-old Dorothy Counts, a young woman who integrated Charlotte, North Carolina's schools and was "reviled and spat upon by the mob." The combination of close-up photographs of Counts' harassment and Baldwin's voice makes visceral her pain as Baldwin narrates it.

> There was unutterable pride, tension and anguish in that girl's face as she approached the halls of learning with history jeering at her back. It made me furious. It filled me with both hatred and pity. And it made me ashamed. Some one of us should have been there with her.

And yet this sequence is about the Black woman as catalyst and as image for Baldwin. In this sequence, as with that of the female protestors from the 1960s and in Ferguson – the Black girl/woman is a voiceless often still image – a symbol of protest and its perils rather than an articulate, daily worker in the struggle for freedom as Martin, Malcolm, and Medgar are. Further, the composite image of the Black community that emerges from Peck's film is predominantly male, a fact that would make more sense if Peck directly addressed masculinity as part of the phenomenon he is analyzing.

I Am Not Your Negro deserves consideration in the broader sphere of contemporary Black independent and documentary filmmaking, an arena that shows increasing internal polarization about how and whether to address intersectional approaches to identity and to revolution. Indeed, these films raise the question of whether a film can really be revolutionary if it is not attentive to intersectional dimensions. Doesn't one man's revolution become too easily an act of domination to another – particularly when that "other" is a woman?

The relative absence of Black women in Peck's film comes into striking relief when it is considered alongside *Whose Streets?* (2017), Sabaah Folayan and Damon Davis's documentary about Ferguson, Missouri, in which the intimate and the public life of activism are revealed through a young, queer mother of color, Brittany Ferrell. While the documentary is on its face concerned with detailing Ferguson's activism, it is at its most revelatory when Ferrell, who is one of the film's central activists, states,

> loving a Black woman has to be one of the most beautiful things I have ever done, next to bringing a life into this world. I think about it every single day. It is one of the best decisions I have ever made.

Her statement points to the links between public and private activism – to what the film's protagonists dub "revolutionary love." What about Baldwin's "revolutionary loves"? Can we fully appreciate the depth and complexity of his political contributions if we, as Peck does in *I Am Not Your Negro*, keep Baldwin's sexuality out of the conversation about Black revolutionary politics? There is something powerful about Baldwin's claim of "love" for Malcolm X, a force which casts a queer light over a figure synonymous with Black masculine power and control. But because Peck's film never confirms nor denies Baldwin's sexuality, the power of this love claim may be lost on audiences unfamiliar with Baldwin's sexuality.

Like *Whose Streets?* Damani Baker's documentary, *The House on Coco Road* (2016), in which transnational, Black radical activism is passed down from *mother* to son is an example of contemporary Black intersectional documentary. It is the story of the filmmaker's mother, Black radical activist Fannie Houghton, a comrade of Angela and Fania Davis's who later, seeking freedom and self-determination, moved to Grenada to work with Maurice Bishop's New Jewel movement. Bishop's Marxist revolutionary movement successfully overtook Grenada in the late 1970s but was undone by internal dissension after Ronald Reagan, fearing the island's possible alliance with Cuba and military potential, destabilized the nation. Later, after Bishop was executed, Reagan seized on the instability to invade and kill many New Jewel movement activists including many of Houghton's friends and comrades. Rather than merely resisting or critiquing the limits of masculinist approaches to Black power, Baker quietly uncovers the Black feminist, intimate roots behind Black American revolution that often go unnoticed or unremarked upon. All of the Black American radical figures he covers – Fannie Houghton, Angela Davis, Fania Davis, and Charlene Mitchell – are Black working women who were skilled organizers, many of whom not only organized but also mentored and provided the foundational community-level work for the larger political engagements like the "Free Angela Davis" movement. As Baker traces his family history, it becomes clear that what at first seemed an understated story of his family's migration from the South to California to Grenada is not only a story of migration for rights and opportunity but also a story of the female "organic intellectuals" who have always fostered Black American revolutionary movements.[6]

Early in the film, Baker confronts his mother with insistent questions about why he wasn't told more about their family's past and struggle. His mother – angrily, tearfully – responds with an important truth: "That's the reality. There's a lot we didn't tell you. And we won't. And you'll discover stuff but if we see that, in your interpretation of that discovery, it will hit you in a bad space, we'll speak up." Like Peck's film, Baker's centers on excavating Black radical knowledge. But Baker boldly centers this knowledge not in the public icon but rather in a figure unfamiliar to the discourse: the Black mother. His film reveals the ways in which Black radical knowledge is shrouded – even shuttered – in the protective logic of maternal love. Importantly, Houghton does not ultimately ignore or leave unanswered her son's questions. Rather, she insists that the knowledge be contextualized with empathy, as the protected son becomes the bearer of knowledge and activist legacy: "I took my young children out of my country [USA] to come here [Grenada] and help this country. I left in pain and this is the first time I've been back. So, you've got to be very sensitive," she implores. In this powerful moment, we see a Black activist fighting on both the domestic and the political front, as her maternal desire to protect comes in conflict with her dawning understanding that her son's desire to take up that political work will require more knowledge than protection.

Black women are not only the revolutionaries at the center of this film, but they are the keepers of revolutionary histories. Baker carefully retraces the radical model his mother has drawn, hears her story, and repeats her words on the soundtrack. He constructs his own sense of freedom through the vestiges she leaves. The film's overall refrain that the personal is political, popularized in second wave feminist discourse, takes on additional meaning as we understand it in terms of not only gender but also race, class, and national politics and across generational divides. "Our family's lives were defined by how we defended ourselves against his [Ronald Reagan's] policies," Baker states. Baker's film suggests that it is only through understanding the intersectional complexity of revolution – through the impact of American national policy on a particular Black family – that we can begin to understand institutional racism's insidious hold on Black domesticity. Next to the specific, intimate work that Baker's film accomplishes, *I Am Not Your Negro* seems to rest on, at best, a composite or, at worst, a generalization about Black America, a montage of scattered images of the nation sutured to a single prophetic voice rather than a flesh and blood examination of the trenches of struggle. In part, it is the absence of gender and sexuality in Peck's film that obscures the everyday aching joints and cracking bones of those laboring for freedom on multiple fronts.

Since 2016 there have been a number of films that challenge white supremacy as practiced against the Black male body, but from an intersectional standpoint. In *Strong Island* (2017), Yance Ford erects a powerful memorial to his brother, whose death at the hands of a white assailant had multiple witnesses but was judged noncriminal by a grand jury that refused to allow the case to go to trial. Ford's experimental elegy latches on, like Peck's, to everyday objects; in Ford's case, these objects are associated with suburban life – the sprinkler on the lawn, the car necessitated by tract living, and even the mantlepiece photo that becomes the key to unlocking Ford's grief. *Strong Island* denaturalizes these objects, exploring visually how the tragedy of his brother's death – and the injustice of the state's refusal to recognize it as either tragic or criminal – has distorted these things as it has disrupted his family's suburban hopes and dreams. Ford's own experience as a transgender human (like the nonbinary gender of the protagonists in *Whose Streets?*) is not integral to the documentary's storyline. However, Ford's activism is similarly intimate and tied to his family's tragedy.

Strong Island subverts the tropes of family documentaries: while the film ostensibly tells a domestic story, as Ford stages encounters through family photographs with his past, it becomes as much an experiment with visualizing coping with loss – facing the void – as it is about telling his brother's story. It is as much about rupture as it is about narrative. The film begins in the dark, with an abstract sound that it refuses to explain – a repeated thud, which could be knocking on a door or a wall or even hammering into a wall. Then, it reveals a little, a sliver of light that pulses and releases dust in rhythm with the thuds. Then the film cuts to black. Following this, Yance has a conversation with the prosecutor who helped to refuse his brother's crime at trial. He, with guarded politeness and apparent apprehension of the denial likely to follow, asks the prosecutor to "answer some of the questions that have been plaguing me for the last 22 years." This opening exemplifies the cinematic strategy used throughout (Figure 3.1).

Ford's dulled visuals and slow, languished pace combine with the elegiac, silence-punctuated soundtrack to drench the viewer in the depressive affect and experience of his particular kind of grief – a grief held perversely in the chokehold of institutional denial of the injustice of Black death – grief held at bay by American denial of Black equality and humanity. This is a theme Peck also explores. Yet Yance's

Figure 3.1 Strong Island (Yance Ford, 2017).

identification with his lost brother, his living "in the wake," causes the audience to encounter the gendered complexities of grieving: masculinity itself is structured against the very fragility that Ford stages for the audience.[7] So, while Ford's film is not centrally about gender, it – like *Whose Streets?* – uses the experimental documentary format to suggest that revolution is happening – and must happen – not just in the streets but also at home. In so doing, it undermines the tropes of Black masculinity as usual, tropes that are upheld and left unexamined in Peck's film. Both *I Am Not Your Negro* and *Strong Island* lament the public killing of Black men. But while Peck's film does complicate the image of Malcolm X and Martin Luther King, suggesting their fragility, it nevertheless refuses to examine the construction of Black masculinity – to unmask it as dissemblance. Ford's film, by contrast, through its emoting male protagonist, counters the expected tropes of Black masculinity. And Ford's film also gives voice to the Black women (particularly Yance's mother) who witness Black men's deaths in a way that Peck's film does not.

Peck might have gained something, too, from Tracey Heather Strain's *Lorraine Hansberry: Sighted Eyes/Feeling Heart* (2017) – which, like Peck's, is an historical documentary and a literary biography – though it goes even further than *Whose Streets?* in naturalizing the lesbian identity of its subject. Though Hansberry's homosexuality, unlike Baldwin's, was closeted, Strain's documentary reveals the ways that her identification as a lesbian shaped her writing (she wrote lesbian-focused stories under

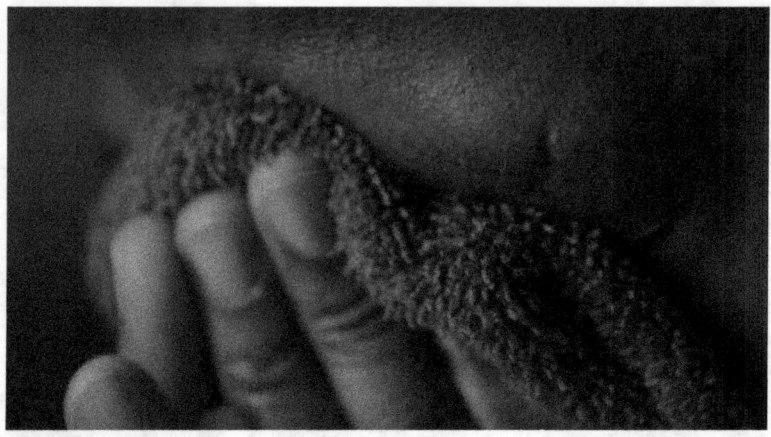

Figure 3.2 Lorraine Hansberry: Sighted Eyes/Feeling Heart (Tracey Heather Strain, 2017).

an assumed name, published in *One* and *The Ladder*). The film does not have the same experimental aesthetics as many of the others of this moment. But Strain rightly recognized that Hansberry's voice itself, properly mounted and quoted, is enough of a resplendent, experimental object to support the film (Figure 3.2).

Baldwin wrote of Hansberry, "Her going did not so much make me lonely as it made me realize how lonely we were," a statement that could be read to reveal their shared situation as queer Black artists in the 1950s and early 1960s. How might Peck's film have looked if he had embraced this loneliness as a part of his project of revealing Baldwin's voice? Strain's film does more than reveal Hansberry as a lesbian. It, like Ford's film, exposes the biological grain of the turmoil that is at the center of so many Black lives. Whether it is Hansberry's father's brain hemorrhage, Hansberry's own cancer, or, in *Strong Island,* Ford's heaving body in grief before the stilted, lifeless camera, the films showcase the struggle with, against, and to surmount one's embattled body as a central issue in Black life. As Baldwin wrote of Hansberry on her deathbed, "She tried to speak, she couldn't. She did not seem frightened or sad, only exasperated that her body no longer obeyed her." The inability to get the body to obey – to do and be right, to conform, confirm or perform – is a central but de-emphasized aspect of the Black freedom struggle. We may not be able to see the racism, sexism, and homophobia that killed Hansberry, as we saw the killing of Malcolm

X or Eric Garner, but that does not mean it was any less lethal. It is the everyday melodrama of wilting – of the body closing in on itself due to institutionally foreclosed possibilities – to which Hansberry, the revolutionary, fell victim.

The ambivalent politics of gender in experimental, Black documentary format is evinced in Terrance Nance's HBO series, *Random Acts of Flyness* (2018–present). Nance's earlier *An Oversimplification of Her Beauty* (2012) is a beautiful work of art. However, it was perhaps unwittingly host to underlying, under-examined gender resentments that risked robbing the titular "her" at the film's center of her voice. By contrast, *Random Acts* is markedly gender-aware. A video game in which a Black woman racks up points for shooting Black men who try to step to her on the street and a sequence where, in an absurdist turn, a police officer (played by Whoopi Goldberg) requires a female assault victim to "turn in her pussy" to the police, thus dramatizing the strain the legal system ironically places on the bodies of Black assault victims, show Nance's efforts at empathy for women and his attempt to give his project over to embodying their perspective. Nance includes Black women characters and makes their voices and views more central than in his previous work, even giving space to Black women filmmakers in specific sketches. But male desire lingers as a driving force. The first episode's conversation with a gender-fluid man seems to take special interest (as Spike Lee's 1986 film *She's Gotta Have It* did earlier) in the open relationship, one that has traditionally, though not exclusively, been a male rather than female fantasy. The sequence of Black women at a backyard barbeque balletically levying a comically large number of aluminum soul food trays has tones of both homage and mockery, the latter solidifying when it emerges that the sequence is advertising a product that allows Black women to snatch their men's roaming thoughts away and thus turns on a joke as old as Sapphire about Black women being controlling. And while female nudity is a repeated feature of the show, male frontal nudity is absent.

While Nance's show, like Peck's film, seems haunted by the learned trappings of Black male desire as we know it, one can nevertheless see Nance struggling against this socialization. His work is entrenched in cross-gender dialogue. He is sharpest and most cutting when he is drawing attention to the juridical, commanding, non-dialogic voices that pepper the soundtrack and internal monologues of Black American life – voice-of-God narration, the commercial announcer (played in his show by Jon Hamm), the voice of the dictionary, and even the voices of actual judges. Through these, Nance draws attention to and reappropriates these largely white, male voices, intrinsically questioning their meaning and sometimes usurping their authority, and by extension, stripping whiteness – and most often white masculinity – of its normalizing power. Likewise, Nance's work is politically at its best when he is less the juridical voice and more the flailingly unsure trickster – experimenting on the edges of his own knowledge, recasting learned gender norms and oppressions in a light that denormalizes Black masculinity. Unlike some Black artists, he does not ignore or depart from the "everyday" in his working-class roots and the ideological baggage these roots entail; he takes on the project, if stutteringly, of "fixing [his] father's father's faults," imagining Black men catcalling each other, hugging, and even, eventually – climactically – erotically embracing. Though still moored in heterosexual premises and axioms, Nance productively stays enmeshed in the intersectional work of overcoming male privilege while recognizing the toll of white supremacy on his own life and body.

What if *I Am Not Your Negro* had, like *Random Acts of Flyness,* experimented with gender as it does with form? One of the powers of experimental documentary is that it unfixes our sense of what visual evidence makes up the human story. Narrative cinema teaches us to follow the bodies on-screen with our eyes, minds, and yearnings; experimental cinema leaves us awash in light and shadow and forces us to reexamine the phenomenon of viewing itself. It points to the cinema's constructedness and materiality and to human life's inertial drive toward abstraction, the nonfigural, and the amorphous. The emphasis on abstraction in the work of the Black media-makers mentioned above has the potential to unravel the taut binding of skin, identity, and personal narrative, suggesting the many things beyond the human form and the talking head that constitute the self and are relevant to history. A ray of light, the sound of knocking, and the grain of a photograph take on as much weight as the human voice, in this way expanding our ways of knowing human experience. What a shame to experiment with cinematic form – to open up our perception of the porousness of Black human experience – only to reify the primacy of the body's socially constructed gender norms. If Peck, whose documentary also experiments with form, had taken on the work of exploring sexuality and gender as Nance does – deciding that it wasn't too much but was instead necessary to the project of understanding the very masculinity Baldwin wrote about in *Remember This House* – the depth of the film's honesty and power would have been greater.

Media authors, like Sabaah Folayan, Damon Davis, Tracy Heather Strain, Yance Ford, Damani Davis, and Terrance Nance, recognize that reconceptualization and reconstitution of Black womanhood and manhood – the burning down of the politics of respectability that haunts representations of Black sexuality – is an essential part of the movement for Black freedom and self-making. Baldwin in reality did the work of remaking Black manhood in part through his identification as a gay man and through *Giovanni's Room* with gay men. To occlude the reality of his queerness from the film does a disservice to this work. Are we going to pretend that the only manifestations of racism worth defending against are those perpetrated by police against Black men? Or are we going to see, as many contemporary Black filmmakers do, that identities are fluid and oppressions linked? Will we recognize the struggle against oppression at the level of the intimate, cellular, the skin, the atom – and atomized? Will we see the biological and internalized grain of racial animus that women's stories force us to appreciate?

Central to the decolonizing of Black bodies is not only removing the threat of police mishandling but also reconceptualizing gender binaries and expectations. Compulsory mistreatment and abuse of Black bodies happens not only at the hands of police but at the hands of gender norms that straitjacket humanity and restrict us from being comfort to one another. The white supremacists who take down Black men are only the cringing face of a deeper ideological struggle that involves gender and sexuality intimately. The phrase "Black lives matter" pertains, we must remember, not only to those involved in struggles in the street but also in the home, in the bed, and coming out of the closet. It pertains to the Black lives seeking life (rather than death) and justice, but also those seeking to fully obtain the constitutional guarantee of "liberty, and the pursuit of happiness."

In response to the emergence of Spike Lee in the 1980s as "the African American filmic who has gotten press, media and academic attention to saturation," Black feminist scholars bell hooks and Wahneemah Lubiano both raised significant questions about his work. While Lubiano recognized that "*She's Gotta Have It* and *School Daze* do raise complicated issues despite both films' masculinist representations and the rampant homophobia of *School Daze*," she also noted that the cultural association of Lee's images with "the real" of all-encompassing Black life was dangerous. This, she argued, was in part because of the foreclosure of the deep, humanizing vision characteristic of Lee generally, in the areas of gender and sexuality – intersections and avenues that the broader culture also leaves largely in the dark. She writes, "The deification of Lee as 'truth sayer,' and his production as 'real,' means that the indexing of his selections becomes the 'essence' of 'Black authenticity' and thus impervious to criticism."[8] Similarly and earlier, in 1981, Kathleen Collins critiqued the representation of women in the work of Bill Gunn (her friend and collaborator), Charles Lane, and Charles Burnett in her signal and under-quoted critique "'A Place in Time' and 'Killer of Sheep': Two Radical Definitions of Adventure Minus Women":

> How odd that two films which propose a new kind of freedom within the Black experience never quite extend this freedom to (their) women…In American film terms, the notion of adventure has certainly undergone a Black metamorphosis. Yet how sad that in the end we are still left with stagnant female souls hovering aimlessly around the male universe. How limiting is the idea that only men despair; Woman can only comfort.[9]

Neither Collins' nor Lubiano's critique was a takedown; it was part of a critical dialogue asking for more from these cinematic authors. These women's critiques, bursting with innovation and powerful of-the-moment understanding, unfortunately are largely ignored in the memory of these films. Perhaps if they had been less ignored, Peck might have avoided walking a similar path to these earlier brilliant Black male independent filmmakers whose narratives of Black life (minus women) can never be the full "real" and whose vision of revolution falls trap to binary logics rather than engaging in multi-frontal, human activism. Felling institutional racism requires understanding the sometimes chafing logic and dynamic of interlocking oppressions.

What I witness in Peck's film is both a burning, prophetic commentary on race in America *and* a palpable, though not malicious, vacuum concerning the importance and activism of Black women. In our openly white supremacist political climate, this critique may seem like splitting hairs. But we need to keep sight of the battle lines established before the 2016 election was lost. To forget these gains amidst the worst kind of political distraction would be to truly lose ground. Thus, while Peck's documentary does reveal white privilege's relentless impassivity to Black suffering and white supremacy's everyday logic in (segregated) supermarkets, in the suburban Chevy, or on the (segregated) white picnic, the neglect of Black women is blight and blind spot in its otherwise clarifying political project. In a film essentially about exposing the privilege of neglect and denial that the empowered enjoy, the irony is worth noting.

Notes

1 James Baldwin, "An Open Letter to My Sister, Miss Angela Davis," *The New York Review of Books*, 7 January 1971.
2 "Are the United States One Nation, One Law, One People," interview with Richard Wright in *La Nef,* reprinted in *Conversations with Richard Wright*, ed. Michel Fabre (Jackson: University Press of Mississippi, 1993), 178.

3 James Baldwin, "Sweet Lorraine," *Esquire*, 1 November 1969, 139–140.
4 Combahee River Collective, in *Let Nobody Turn Us Around: Voices of Resistance, Reform, and Renewal: An African American Anthology*, eds. Manning Marable and Leith Mullings (Lanham, MD: Rowman and Littlefield, 2009), 524.
5 See Barbara Ransby, *Ella Baker and the Black Freedom Movement: A Radical Democratic Vision* (Chapel Hill: University of North Carolina Press, 2003) for a discussion of the marginalization of Black women in the civil rights movement. See also the insightful scholarly essays in Bettye Collier-Thomas and V.P. Franklin's *Sisters in the Struggle: African American Women in the Civil Rights-Black Power Movement* (New York: New York University Press, 2001).
6 Gramsci referred to "organic intellectuals" as having a different relationship to the people than traditional intellectuals.

> The mode of being of the new intellectual can no longer consist in eloquence, which is an exterior and momentary mover of feelings and passions, but in active participation in practical life, as constructor, organizer, "permanent persuader" and not just a simple orator (but superior at the same time to the abstract mathematical spirit); from technique-as-work one proceeds to technique-as-science and to the humanistic conception of history, without which one remains "specialized" and does not become "directive" (specialized and political).

Antonio Gramsci, "The Formation of Intellectuals," in *The Prison Notebooks*, eds. Quinten Hoare and Geoffrey Nowell Smith (New York: International Publishers Co, 1989), 10. As George Lipsitz elaborates, organic intellectuals

> lack formal recognition from society that they are engaged in intellectual activity. Traditional intellectuals can distinguish themselves purely through the originality of their ideas or the eloquence of their expression, but organic intellectuals must initiate a process that involves people in social contestation.

George Lipsitz, *Ivory Perry: A Life in the Struggle* (Philadelphia, PA: Temple University Press, 2011), 10.
7 The notion of living in the wake is derived from Christina Sharpe, *In the Wake: On Blackness and Being* (Durham: University of North Carolina Press, 2016), 14.
8 Wahneemah Lubiano, "But Compared to What?: Reading Realism, Representation, and Essentialism in *School Daze*, *Do the Right Thing*, and the Spike Lee Discourse," *Black American Literature Forum* 25, no. 2, Black Film Issue (Summer 1991): 253–282.
9 Kathleen Collins, "'A Place in Time' and 'Killer of Sheep': Two Radical Definitions of Adventure Minus Women," in *In Color: 60 Years of Images of Minority Women in Film...1921–1981*, ed. Pearl Bowser (New York: Third World Newsreel, 1981), 5–7.

4 James Baldwin: *The Price of the Ticket* (1989) and *I Am Not Your Negro* (2016) as historicist documentaries

Stephen Casmier

This chapter examines Raoul Peck's 2016 film *I Am Not Your Negro* and Karen Thorsen's 1989 film *James Baldwin: The Price of the Ticket* as historicist documentaries, in the sense that they are engaged in present acts of recovery that are as much about their charged moments of production as they are about the now iconic figure of James Baldwin. It argues that anyone who has seen both works would come away perplexed by the radically differing portraits of Baldwin and his instability as a historical referent. The earlier documentary, *The Price of the Ticket*, seems engaged in conventional and loving hagiography, allowing the author's own image and voice and those of teary-eyed friends and fellow writers to "set the record straight." Thorsen's film emphasizes Baldwin's importance, his legacy, and his status as one of the giants of African American literature and as a gay icon of the burgeoning identity politics movement, who embraced a message of white transformation and transcendent brotherly love as the foundation for a healing ethic to remedy the original sin of American racism. Conversely, the later film, *I Am Not Your Negro*, presents an angry, prophetic figure – an icon of Black nationalist identity – as it taps into the contemporary state and unfinished business of American racial politics, Black Lives Matter, the rage on the streets of the Ferguson insurgence, and the once again urgent "by-any means-necessary" message of Baldwin's murdered friend, Malcolm X.

These films, therefore, can be seen as *presentist* acts of "recovery" that embrace aspects of Marxist revisionist history and its child "New Historicism," which recognize this fundamental instability of the original historic referent and its contamination by a compounding multiplicity of present moments. According to Louis Montrose, in his 1989 work, *Professing the Renaissance: The Poetics and Politics of Culture*,

> we can have no access to a full and authentic past, a lived material existence, unmediated by the surviving textual traces of the society

in question – traces whose survival we cannot assume to be merely contingent but must rather presume to be at least partially consequent upon complex and subtle social processes of preservation and effacement; and secondly, that those textual traces are themselves subject to subsequent textual mediations when they are construed as the "documents" upon which historians ground their own texts, called "histories."[1]

So, this chapter explores the "subtle social processes of preservation and effacement" at work in 1989 and in 2016, which form the historical context to the production of radically different images of Baldwin. Significantly, the New Historicism Montrose describes in 1989 was one of the emergent, safe, and popularized critical theories that gave license to and ultimately animated the present-oriented "recovery" of Baldwin as the radically different, iconic figure of both documentaries. Through such recovery, the two documentaries thus seem to openly engage and then disseminate the current political positions and theories of their moment of production, presenting the type of tension recently elaborated by Robert Gooding-Williams in his 2017 essay, "History of African American Political Thought and Antiracist Critical Theory." In this essay, Gooding-Williams explores a tension between what he calls the "presentist" and "antiquarian" methodologies in approaching African American history. At issue is whether those who work in critical race theory and anti-racist politics should pursue "presentist" historical projects that read anachronistically, imposing contemporary ideas (and vocabulary) concerning race conflict and racial identity – actively responding to contemporary problems – or whether they should embrace "antiquarian" projects and struggle to get a better understanding of the language, ideas, and thoughts with which the historical figures were working at the time.[2] Meanwhile, "recovery" here refers to the type of preoccupation described by Edward Saïd. In his 1991 article "The Politics of Knowledge," Saïd rails against "the pure politics of identity,"[3] its "ethnic particularity,"[4] "triviality," dogged lamentations that some "*names* were left out," and "flat minded" questions about inclusion.[5] In other words, the films also function as histories of the past 40 years of expanding neoliberal hegemony and expose what happened to the volatile arguments and countercultural politics of the 1960s and 1970s as they became the "identity politics" of the last quarter of the 20th century. The era that begins in the early 1980s is one that transformed and gentrified, for instance, the radical Marxist "identity politics" of groups such as the Combahee River Collective or the Rainbow Coalition of murdered Chicago Black Panther Fred Hampton and his consciousness raising chant: "I am a revolutionary."[6] By the 1980s, "identity politics" began to stand for the particular interest group politics of self-esteem often criticized by intellectuals on the left and the right. Hampton's "I am a revolutionary" became the slogan "I am somebody" from the opportunistic political reformist Jesse Jackson and his rebranding of the original Rainbow Coalition.[7] The films ultimately demonstrate that even the present-oriented Marxist revisionist history of Walter Benjamin, which was once presented as "a revolutionary chance in the fight for the oppressed past," can be transformed into safe acts of historicist recovery that work to serve the present desires for comfort and self-esteem embraced by particularized interest groups.[8]

The Price of the Ticket and the recovery of Baldwin as a gay icon of identity politics

> **Baldwin**: *There are days, this is one of them, when you wonder what your role is in this country and what your future is in it?*
> *From my point of view, no label, and no slogan, and no party, and no skin color, indeed, no religion is more important than the human being.*
> **Interviewer**: *When you were started out as a writer, you were black, impoverished, homosexual. You must have said to yourself: "Gee, how disadvantaged can I get?"*
> **Baldwin**: *No, I thought I hit the jackpot. It was so outrageous, it could not go any further ... so, you had to find a way to use it.*
> —James Baldwin: *The Price of the Ticket*

The Price of the Ticket begins as a mosaic with excerpts from three separate filmed interviews of the author from three different periods of his life, as if to summarize him, his message, his legacy, and his continuing historical significance to viewers of the late 1980s, just after his death. The film is an almost formulaic, biographical documentary that borders on hagiography, with Baldwin, in the words of one of its voices, as a "hero." It was documentary filmmaker Karen Thorsen's first full-length film and was actually supposed to be based on the same manuscript taken up by Raoul Peck nearly 30 years later for *I Am Not Your Negro*. According to Thorsen,

> Our goal was a cinéma-vérité film about the writing of Baldwin's next book. The book, *Remember This House*, was to be Baldwin's memoir of the Civil Rights Era and his friendships with Medgar Evers, Malcolm X and Martin Luther King, Jr. It was to be an

on-camera exploration of history, intercut with three crucial interviews: conversations with the slain leaders' three children, now young adults, whom Baldwin had known since they were kids.[9]

Baldwin, however, died before they could undertake the collaboration, and Thorsen decided to make the documentary about Baldwin instead. According to one reviewer, writing at the time of its release, the result is a "restrained and authentic" work that only deviates from the formulas of the day by eschewing a narrator, which "would be superfluous and intrusive."[10] Indeed, for another reviewer, allowing Baldwin's family, friends, and lovers to tell his story was a somewhat problematic decision for the time – given the complex status of Baldwin's reputation at that moment.

> In order to vary the pace of the narrative Thorsen has drafted in what the credits call "witnesses", who appear as talking heads … of them all only [Lucien] Happersberger – who met Baldwin when aged seventeen in Paris and who was present at his deathbed – gives the impression of appreciating him as a character of flesh and blood. Some of the others seem to be putting him forward as a candidate for plaster sainthood.[11]

Upon its release, gay and lesbian film festivals featured it on their programs.[12] And in 2015, one reviewer called it: "For years the authoritative film biography of James Baldwin."[13]

Watching this film, one is never forced to feel the contingency of the present through the intruding, subjective, and historic position of the filmmaker or through the surrounding and charged moment of its production. The film's primary mission seems to be to perform subtle, revisionist acts of historical inclusion or recovery – much like Isaac Julien's 1988 experimental film, *Looking for Langston*, which also performs a recovery of a particular legacy for Langston Hughes. *The Price of the Ticket* "rescues" Baldwin's legacy as it monumentalizes and transforms him into the type of figure that could be easily embraced by the nascent multiculturalism and charged identity politics movements of the late 1980s – a period besieged by what some have labeled the "culture wars."

And Baldwin needed rescuing. Once, in the early 1960s, Baldwin had come "to embody the voice of 'the Negro'," writes famed African Americanist Henry Louis Gates in a significant 1992 article for *The New Republic Magazine* that sums up the writer's legacy during that period.[14] Yet, Gates writes, "by the late 1960s Baldwin bashing was almost a rite of initiation" among militant African American writers. A "new generation, so it seemed, was determined to define itself by everything Baldwin was not."[15] According to Gates, he was excoriated because of his queer identity. "Young militants," says Gates, "referred to Baldwin, unsmilingly, as Martin Luther Queen."[16] Meanwhile, an unapologetically racist and "a newly sexualized black nationalism" had arisen "that could stigmatize homosexuality as a capitulation to alien white norms, and in that way accredit homophobia as a progressive political act."[17] This all but remained the case until 1992 when, says Gates, "the times had changed; and they have stayed changed."[18] Still at the end of the essay, Gates observes that in the early 1990s, an

> influential black intellectual avant-garde in Britain has resurrected Baldwin as a patron saint, and a new generation of readers has come to value just those qualities of ambivalence and equivocality, just that sense of the contingency of identity, that made him useless to the ideologues of liberation and anathema to so many black nationalists.[19]

Indeed, by the 1990s, the ideas of Black nationalism and the radical counterculture had not fared any better than Baldwin. For instance, in 1974, a group of radical, queer Black feminist women, The Combahee River Collective, published *The Combahee River Collective Statement*, a manifesto embracing a position that they radically branded "identity politics" because they said, "We realize that the only people who care enough about us to work consistently for our liberation are us."[20] The manifesto openly embraced the radical Marxist and anti-capitalist politics of the time, evincing solidarity with all of the "wretched of the earth."

> The most general statement of our politics at the present time would be that we are actively committed to struggling against racial, sexual, heterosexual, and class oppression, and see as our particular task the development of integrated analysis and practice based upon the fact that the major systems of oppression are interlocking.[21]

Yet, with the 1980s and the onset of the Reagan era, "identity politics" as a term had gone on a new gentrifying and revisionist detour that privileged particular identities over shared consciousness.

An agent of that transformation was civil rights activist Jesse Jackson, who made two runs for President of the United States in the 1980s as a leader of a party he called the Rainbow Coalition. Yet, the idea of a

Rainbow Coalition was first the brainchild of the charismatic revolutionary and member of the Black Panther Party, Fred Hampton, who was summarily executed by Chicago Police in 1969. A 1971 *New York Times* article about Hampton noted that he conceptualized the Rainbow Coalition (much like the drafters of the River Collective manifesto) as a "'formal coalition' with the Uptown Young Patriots, a radical group of white Southerners in the Chicago area."[22] In his speeches, Hampton fomented a consciousness for radical class politics as he exhorted crowds to shout with him: "I am a revolutionary!" After Hampton's execution, Jackson stepped into the vacuum and revised Hampton's revolutionary exhortation with a phrase that came to define identity politics as it emphasizes what some critics have called the ethos of "psychic emancipation" over that of revolutionary consciousness. He relentlessly exhorted crowds to shout in unison throughout the 1970s and early 1980s: "I am somebody ... maybe poor ... maybe on welfare ... maybe unemployed ... maybe in jail ... but I am somebody ... soul power."[23] Through Jackson, Black Power became the less threatening "soul power." "Revolutionary" became "somebody." He carried these transformations into his runs for president in the 1980s as he also transformed the radical Marxist identity politics of the River Collective into liberal, interest group politics of self-esteem, political inclusiveness, and integration into the mainstream capitalist economy. He was thus on the vanguard of an intellectual and cultural movement that aggressively took root in the late 1980s and early 1990s. This movement began to privilege particular identities as it embraced the anti-hierarchical bent of post-structuralist theory; helped precipitate the rise of cultural studies, feminist studies, ethnic studies, deconstruction, and queer studies; and ignited debates about the value of the western canon and teaching works by "dead white men" instead of recovering the lost and marginalized voices of the oppressed. In her 1990 article, "Humanities for the Future: Reflections on the Western Culture Debate at Stanford," Mary Louise Pratt emphasizes Jackson's influence on what has come to be known as the "culture wars" and the debate over the curriculum at elite universities such as Stanford. "Student momentum began to coalesce during the Rainbow Coalition activity for the 1984 election and through the intense antiapartheid activity of 1985–86."[24]

It is thus easy to see *The Price of the Ticket* as emanating from a late 1980s context that enabled the recovery of Baldwin as an icon of the emergent, neoliberal identity politics movement. The documentary sounds all of the important themes that would give Baldwin currency in the contentious times of its production. It foregrounds the multicultural "jackpot" of his identity as "black, impoverished, homosexual."

Yet, it also paradoxically presents Baldwin as a strident believer in the type of then-suspect, humanist ethos of transcendent universal brotherhood that also undermines reified and discreet notions of identity that were taking root in the 1980s (Figure 4.1). "From my point of view," a black and white image of Baldwin states at the opening of the documentary, "no label, and no slogan, and no party, and no skin color, indeed, no religion is more important than the human being".

These interviews set the tone of the documentary, which then switches to footage of Baldwin's 1987 funeral at the Cathedral of Saint John the Divine in New York City. All of beautiful, brilliantly dressed Black Harlem seems to be in attendance, in addition to major figures of the African American literary scene. Among the attendees, one can pick out photographer Gordon Parks, activist Kwame Ture (Stokely Carmichael), novelist Toni Morrison, poet Amiri Baraka (LeRoi Jones), and Maya Angelou. The film conveys the impression that it is a remarkable event for a major African American figure. According to African American film scholar Clyde Taylor, who attended the funeral, more than 5,000 people filled the church. Among them was jazz drummer

Figure 4.1 Cosmopolitan Baldwin, *James Baldwin: The Price of the Ticket* (Karen Thorsen, 1989).

Max Roach, who said, "You writers sure know how to put somebody away."[25]

Then, the film cuts to the image and recognizable voice of Maya Angelou delivering a eulogy at the church before later sitting down for the camera and tearfully describing Baldwin and his impact while sometimes reading from his work. Indeed, throughout the documentary, when filmed images of Baldwin do not allow him to speak for himself, Angelou's voice often becomes his as she dramatically reads from his fiction and essays. It is a choice that resonates in a multiplicity of ways with the film's recovery of Baldwin. Indeed, in 2012, one poet described the actual *gravitas* of Angelou, whose "persona far outweighs her accomplishments in my consciousness"[26] and thus subtly locates her within the emergent caricature of the type of identity politics icon that was still inchoate and hotly debated in the late 1980s:

> Maya Angelou is the quintessential role model. She embodies the major themes that preoccupied twentieth century America: (1) overcoming adversity, (2) making victimhood a position of strength, and (3) celebrating one's heritage. At a moment when many writers were focused on the impossibility of communication through language, Angelou was focused on making her own letters crystal clear—and it won her an audience that included President Clinton.[27]

Eventually, Angelou became one of the most famous African Americans in the country after she read her poem, "On the Pulse of Morning," at the January 1993 presidential inauguration of fellow Arkansan, Bill Clinton.[28] Indeed, by the late 1990s, it was all too easy for comedian David Alan Grier, to dress up in a campy, drag version of Angelou for *Saturday Night Live* skits and parody her voice, dramatically pitching Butterfingers, Froot Loops, and Hallmark Greeting Cards.

These skits, which in some ways serve more curiously as pastiche than parody, capture an important aspect of Angelou's voice and dramatic self-presentation that also leaks into *The Price of the Ticket* through her reading of Baldwin's work. The skits underscore Angelou's self-consciously urbane and sophisticated self-presentation and voice (as it is linked to James Baldwin's similar voice), which goes against the grain of the populist and more "Black" voice and language urgently embraced by late 1960s activists and Black cultural nationalists. At that time, conveying a distinctly Black voice was a major agenda of militant Black writers, who favored a voice that would resist "elitist tendencies," "reach and reflect common Black folks," and embrace the

"Black idiom" by capturing "the flavor of Black American speech – its rhythms and sounds, both its dialect and style," asserts African American linguist Geneva Smitherman in 1973.[29] Yet, in *The Price of the Ticket*, the accented voices of Angelou and Baldwin mostly defy this idiom, its rhythmic patterns, syntax, verbal style, and above all what Smitherman lists as its "intonation patterns, tonal qualities and other aspects of Black phonology." The somewhat Europeanized lilt of Baldwin's voice (drawing it away from the vernacular tonalities in fashion in the late 1960s and 1970s), coupled with Angelou's theatrical, powerfully interpretive, and distinctly gendered reading of it, reproduces some of the sexual tensions that famously triggered the homophobia of certain militants and led to Baldwin's near submergence in the following decades. According to a 1989 critique of the film by *New York Times* columnist Walter Goodman, "Readings from Baldwin's best-known essays and fiction, somewhat affectedly delivered by Maya Angelou, tie his life and work together."[30] Through Angelou, *The Price of the Ticket* recovers the grain and queer resonance of Baldwin's voice.

In fact, by the late 1980s, something was changing in the spirit of the times that helped in the recovery of Baldwin and his elevation from the margins as a queer figure. Indeed, despite Baldwin's own denunciation of gay politics and a gay identity, Baldwin scholar Douglas Field observes in 2004 that many queer African American writers had come to view him as "an inspiration" and "progenitor of many of the theoretical formulations currently associated with feminist, gay, and gender studies" who "helped rip the hinges off the closet."[31] By the late 1980s, Field notes, criticism "began to argue for Baldwin's central place, not only as an important African-American writer, but as a black and gay artist."[32] What helped, argues another Baldwin scholar, Dwight McBride, is the emergence of new scholarship that enabled thinkers to reassess the "complicated relationships … between race, gender, class and sexuality."[33] The same year *The Price of the Ticket* came out, Eve Kosofsky Sedgwick published her groundbreaking book *Epistemology of the Closet*, which posited sexuality as a foundation for a distinct identity, going against Baldwin's assertion in a 1984 interview that the word gay "answers a false argument, a false accusation."[34]

Consequently, *The Price of the Ticket* goes in search of, restores, and revitalizes the Baldwin legend as well as the marginalized and suppressed Jimmy – the gay Jimmy. It partially recovers that legend through praise-filled interviews with the standard talking heads of conventionalized documentary. And, like *Looking for Langston*, the overall effect of the documentary is one of contingently breathing life into the aspects of the writer's life that were hidden in plain sight – his gay and cosmopolitan side as taken up by the voice of Angelou and then reinforced by the testimony of a theater performer, a dancer and personal assistant, a cabaret singer, a few Turkish actors, a Harlem barman (his brother David), and a former lover emerging from the shadows (Happersberger). Finally, out of the closet and without shame, these figures belt out old spirituals, cry in remembrance, speak of late nights and bouts of drinking until morning, and give voice to the particular love – of *eros* (bodily love) and *philia* (brotherly love) – denounced in the late 1960s as the actual but hidden foundation for the *agape* (selfless and universal love for humanity) brazenly disseminated by Baldwin's early writings. The background is radical activist Eldridge Cleaver's widely popular 1968 book *Soul on Ice*, wherein he cruelly denounces Baldwin's sophisticated style and open homosexuality as conveying a deep self-hatred and specific love for white men that merely masquerades as an integrationist and transcendent ethic of brotherly love. He asserts, "Indirectly Baldwin was defending his first love – the white man."[35] Then, he adds, "Baldwin has a superb touch when he speaks of human beings, when he is inside of them – especially his homosexuals – but he flounders when he looks beyond the skin."[36] *The Price of the Ticket* displays this love without shame. "We were in love with each other, you know," asserts a teary-eyed Happersberger, the Swiss painter who brought Baldwin to his home in the Alps where the writer finished his first published novel, *Go Tell It on the Mountain*. "We must have been a very strange couple in that village," he says. This is reinforced by Angelou, who, after reading an excerpt from one of Baldwin's novels, presents her own summary of it: "*Another Country* is about black and whites trying to connect; trying to respect each other; trying desperately to love each other."

I Am Not Your Negro and the recovery of James Baldwin as a radical figure of Black politics

In June 1979, acclaimed author James Baldwin commits to a complex endeavor: tell his story of America through the lives of three of his murdered friends:
Medgar Evers
Martin Luther King Jr
Malcolm X
Baldwin never got past his 30 pages of notes entitled: Remember This House

—I Am Not Your Negro

I Am Not Your Negro can also be viewed as a presentist act of recovery: the recovery of a lost manuscript and of Baldwin's identity as a radical Black man that places him in the company of Malcolm X, while distancing him from what one literary critic called the late 1960s "rite" of "Baldwin bashing,"[37] and a young militant's denunciation of him as a fawning, color-struck gay "boy, with a white mind"[38] that all but destroyed the reputation and political cachet of the writer for the next 20 years. At first glance, Peck's work seems to be entering into the discursive field of revisionist Baldwin biography, performing its own, present-oriented act of recovery, perhaps with the image of Baldwin from *The Price of the Ticket* as its foil. Both films use many of the same archival images and media clips. Yet, *I Am Not Your Negro* seems to begin as a gloss on the translation of Baldwin's universal love or *agape* into the *eros* of particular love for white men. It starts with dramatic music and text scrolling onto a split, black-and-white screen – as if being written in the moment by the writer's typewriter – explaining the telegraphed and doggedly present-focused origins of the documentary. The words announce the agenda of the film, which is to breathe new life into those 30 pages written 40 years ago. Then, the scene switches to Baldwin, in color, being interviewed in a 1968 episode of the nationally televised *The Dick Cavett Show*. It presents the image of Cavett as small, blondish, and vulnerable – one of the first public figures in America to openly admit he suffered from clinical depression. Against this, the clip showcases Baldwin as lithe, brilliant, outspoken, and a bit disheveled. Both men are famous and seem sheepishly to struggle to contain a smile over some hidden secret not known to viewers as Baldwin responds to the talk show host's question about why Negroes aren't more hopeful. Baldwin refuses to take the bait or assume the position projected by what he characterizes as Cavett's "peculiar language," which is the language of host and guest, of perpetrator and victim, of interviewer and interviewee, of dominant and submissive. Instead, he tussles with Cavett, resorting to his well-known (and by then rejected) discourse of mutuality, prophetically saying, "It's not a question of what happens to the negro here, or the black man here. That's a very good question for me, but the real question is 'what's going to happen to this country?'" The film then confirms Baldwin's prophetic warning as it smoothly shifts to a contemporary montage of similarly colored photographs of Black Lives Matter and Ferguson protestors being assaulted, handled, and threatened with guns by police to the music of Buddy Guy singing "Damn Right I've Got the Blues" in the music's famous AABB endlessly repeating, circular style. Through such a style, the music and the images thwart the pastness of the past, invoking what theorist Walter

Benjamin calls the immemorial "presence of the now [Jetztzeit],"[39] reminding viewers of and making obscenely present the violent protest taking place on the streets at the time of the film's production, compelling them to layer it onto the upheaval following the assassination of Martin Luther King in 1968, perhaps the background to that episode of *The Dick Cavett Show*.

Along with the title, *I Am Not Your Negro*'s beginning suggests not only a new, emergent, and radical present but a different recovered image of Baldwin, implying that he is not the figure of *The Price of the Ticket*, that his sexual identity is not paramount, and that, above all, he is not Dick Cavett's "negro." It places Baldwin in the service of the "now," of a filmmaker in synthetic accord with current Black identity politics and the ongoing violent and existential threat to African American life in the United States (Figure 4.2).

After the title credits, the film then turns to more words progressing across the screen to the sound of a typewriter, and then shifts to a contemporary urban landscape with the camera slowly panning beneath elevated railway tracks as a low, simmering voice reads a 1979 letter by Baldwin to the Spartan Literary Agency proposing the forgotten work. This voice is in marked contrast to Baldwin's own urban-sophisticate voice and that of Maya Angelou, which stood in for Baldwin's in *The Price of the Ticket*. Peck has chosen African American actor Samuel L. Jackson to read words from the 30 pages of Baldwin's writing, a loaded choice. In many ways, his voice is diametrically opposed to that of

Figure 4.2 Prophetic Baldwin, *I Am Not Your Negro* (Raoul Peck, 2016).

Angelou, though, like her, he is preternaturally recognizable. He is currently one of the most bankable stars in Hollywood. In interviews, Jackson has said that he was active in the civil rights and Black Power movements, was once addicted to drugs, and has a prison record. Meanwhile, his *Internet Movie Data Base* page observes that he has a "[d]eep and authoritative voice" playing characters who are "prone to intimidation or violence," have "great capacities for violence," "swear a lot," and are "hotheaded [...] with a fiery temper." In interviews, Peck said that he wanted all of these things when he chose Jackson to perform Baldwin. "We were not looking for someone to mimic Baldwin's incomparable voice but more to give it a new life, a new strength and even more, remarkable selflessness."[40] In another interview, Peck states,

> I knew a famous name would help. But, I also wanted not only a great actor but somebody who has some sort of street credibility; somebody we could trust when we heard his voice [...] So, it had to be somebody who in his real life had some sort of grounded attitude and respect [...] when you hear him speak about himself, his life, who he is, or about political issues he's always clear about it. That I liked.[41]

Peck therefore chose a figure of the immediate present for contemporary film audiences, who might instantly recognize his ubiquitous voice (he has 186 credits for films), which brings with it an aura of "street credibility" and all of the potential explosiveness of contemporary Black life.

So, *I Am Not Your Negro* first presents as a revision of the revision, as it brings back the once almost discarded, disremembered (yet paradoxically overdetermined) image of James Baldwin and the African American writer's own aborted attempt at remembering and revising the 1960s assassinations of his friends: Malcolm X, Martin Luther King, and Medgar Evers. The film is based on fragments of a story that Baldwin did not finish (or maybe could not tell) as he entered a late midlife crisis following the hope and despair of the 1960s. According to Peck's introduction to his book about the film, one day, Baldwin's sister Gloria Karefa-Smart handed him "a packet of some thirty pages of letters called 'Notes Toward Remember This House,' a book project that James Baldwin never finished."[42] Then, Peck describes an unconventional project that is perhaps more genre-defying art film than historic documentary: "A book that was never written. That's the story."[43] Next, he presents his and Baldwin's ragged aesthetic craft, assembling the film from "several pages of notes typed, in no particular format, containing erasures, the object of repeated corrections," and handles these as the found-objects of a quilt-like "precious mosaic."[44] The film thus foregrounds its own fragmented form, as it consists of an assemblage of documents that (in her contribution to the book about the film) the film's editor, Alexandra Strauss, lists as "photos, old movies, newsreels, newspaper headlines, advertisements, [...] amateur videos, all in different formats and styles" and "the films Baldwin saw – the films that shaped his own mythology, that framed his childhood and marked him."[45]

If seen as revisionist history, the effect of the film is staggering. It overflows with the despair of the moment and the pronouncements from the immemorial past of an aging prophet. At one point, for instance, Jackson reads Baldwin's prophetic words over a clip from Gus Van Sant's *Elephant* (2003) and the distinctive sounds of a cocking gun, a shot, and the screaming of a young woman that restage the murders at Columbine High School in 1999. "To look around the United States today is enough to make prophets and angels weep." Indeed, within this film, many of the passages from Baldwin's work depart from the voices and memories of his teary-eyed friends captured by *The Price of the Ticket*. There are no conventionalized talking heads in this film. Meanwhile, Baldwin questions his earlier persona and laments: "I was in some way in those years, without entirely realizing it, the Great Black Hope of the great white father." Furthermore, there is little of the universalizing and humanist hope – "the Great Black Hope" – of reconciliation through the psychic emancipation of identity politics. Instead, the film moves James Baldwin and Martin Luther King, Jr., much closer to the Black nationalist ideas of Malcolm X, who often expressed the idea that change would only come about through violent confrontation. "Malcolm was one of the people Martin saw on the mountaintop," Baldwin says cryptically in the unfinished work about his friends. He then acknowledges that he and Malcolm X "were simply trapped in the same situation." The film thus resounds with a sense of imminent catastrophe. The obvious cumulative effect of the work and its arrangement of sound and image is the emergence of a figure captured by such potent words as "trapped," "bitter," "enemy," "vengeance," and "helpless rage." "Well, I am tired," Jackson's reading voice intones. "I don't know how it will come about. But no matter how it comes about it will be bloody. It will be hard."

By comparing the "presentist" orientation of the two films and excavating some of the contentious political arguments contextualizing their moments of production, it is easy to see a certain ebb and flow of radically different performances of the historic recovery of the same figure. This is made possible by a certain conception of history anchored in the methodology of Marxist revisionist history translated into safe, inclusive acts of recovery. Yet, like many of the radical ideas of the 20th century, this presentist orientation, along with radical identity politics, underwent a detour of translation, transformation, and gentrification in the age of neoliberalism. Both *The Price of the Ticket* and *I Am Not Your Negro* seem to embody this continuing state of affairs. Both engage in history relentlessly bound by western epistemology and its dogmatic structuring through language or the ordering dictatorship of signs, symbols, and unstable referents explored and elaborated by the popular post-structuralist thinkers of the late 20th century.

Reclamation: James Baldwin as a mystery of Black Atlantic cosmology

While *The Price of the Ticket* anchors itself in the conventions of formulaic documentary, *I Am Not Your Negro* self-consciously grapples with its aesthetic form. Although a document of historic recovery, *The Price of the Ticket* still attempts to masquerade as somewhat objective history as it anchors itself in convention, without self-reflexivity. For example, when it uses the now hackneyed convention of what has been infamously called the "Ken Burns" effect – panning across or zooming into archival photographs – it seems to do this for the sake of the viewers' comfort, producing motion where there is none, pandering to projected assumptions about their infamous short attention spans. *I Am Not Your Negro*, however, craftily uses this same convention to produce discomfort as it pans across and zooms with enraged deliberateness into the once banalized images of Jim Crow society at once highlighting white normativity and its production of "the Negro" as a grotesque inferior being. Furthermore, while *I Am Not Your Negro* also seems to masquerade as a historical document, the somewhat eclectic structure of the film appears to borrow from Peck's other, more experimental work, notably his haunting film: *Lumumba: La mort du prophète* (1990). In his 2011 essay, on Peck's work, "Raoul Peck's *Lumumba* and *Lumumba: La mort du prophète*: On Cultural Amnesia and Historical Erasure, " cultural critic Burlin Barr describes how that film aesthetically moves through the double binds of performing history, noting that the "primary structure and conceptual terrain" of *La mort du prophète*" is "to confront the symbolic structures of erasure, rather than to present a hagiography or to reconstruct a historical record."[46] This indeed places *I Am Not Your Negro* squarely in the company of New Historicist histories, which, according to Montrose, are subjected to such self-conscious "textual mediations."[47]

Yet, in his own description of the form of *I Am Not Your Negro* for the book, Peck reveals that he did not model the film on other documentaries or western aesthetic paradigms. Instead, he says, he wanted the work to follow James Baldwin's lead and aspire to cook up through the film "a funky dish of chitterlings."[48] Indeed, as has been stated, he further compares the original text with its absence of structure, "erasures" and "repeated corrections" to the found-objects of a "precious mosaic."[49] This type of aesthetic structure evokes the bundles and containers of Black Atlantic and Haitian cosmology. And this would lead the film paradoxically to appear as both representation and the thing-in-and-of-itself as it deploys the techniques and technology of film to work the mysteries of Black Atlantic craft subtly substituting the "recovery" of James Baldwin with his "reclamation."

In experiencing *I Am Not Your Negro* as such an object, it is thus possible to sense that it is not only *about* history or a historic moment, but it can also be an *act* of stripping away history through an aesthetic feat that resembles (or deploys) what the practitioners of Haitian Voudoun call "reclamation."[50] Through this awareness, the film transforms into another type of vessel – a *govi*[51] – one which doesn't recover Baldwin's spirit as a cultural icon but "reclaims" it (*retirer d'en bas de l'eau*). For the practitioners of Haitian Voudoun, this is a powerful act that ultimately begins the process of releasing the guiding and possessing spirits – the *mystères* or *loas* – of the race. In her influential work, *Divine Horsemen: The Living Gods of Haiti* (1953), Maya Deren describes this as a three-step process. It begins with the reclamation of the soul – the *gros bon ange* – a "precious accumulation" which is "the repository of a man's history, his form, and his force, the final resultant of his ability, his intelligence and experience" – from the depths of death or the deep water.[52] This distinct essence or spirit is then purified by divorcing it from the historical remembering of a particular person. According to Deren, "There is no loa who can be remembered by a human being."[53] Interestingly, *I Am Not Your Negro* does not present the usual talking heads or weeping images of friends and scholars engaging in such acts of memory. The "service for ancestral dead," says Deren, "is not a nostalgia or sentimentality."[54] Then, through the process of reclamation, "the person becomes principle," and then, this "abstraction, to function in reality, must become reality. *The principle must become a person*."[55] If this essence is like others, it joins with the pantheon of recognizable loa. If it is radically distinct, as was Baldwin's, it becomes a new *mystère* or loa and a guiding spirit that transcends that of the original ancestral figure. According to Deren: "Unlike the mere ancestral spirit which must be passed down... the loa are part of the very blood of the race and are inherited automatically."[56]

> Where there was once a person, there is now a personage. Transposed to this dimension the summoned voice in the govi [the spiritual container] is no longer intimate, advisory; it is an objective oracular

authority that booms as if from the bowels of the earth. What was once believed is now believed in. He who was once respected is now revered. Where once the parent inspired filial devotion the deity now exacts dedication. The ancestor has been transfigured into a god.[57]

Yet loas are not waiting to be remembered, recovered, sensitively included, or even revered and worshipped. Through acts of reclamation which may ultimately lead to their timeless liberation, they become physically active agents within the world. As such, they are powerful servants of the living who may be called upon to effect change. Says Deren, "it is the duty of loa to intervene."[58]

The loa often acts in the present world as it "mounts" or possesses a person.[59] Even in life, Baldwin had this power. In a eulogy to the writer, African American poet Amiri Baraka describes such spiritual possession, proclaiming Baldwin

> the creator of contemporary American speech even before Americans could dig that. He created it so we could speak to each other at unimaginable intensities of feeling, so we could make sense to each other at higher and higher tempos.[60]

In his 1992 *The New Republic* article, Henry Louis Gates underscores his own possession by Baldwin:

> Eventually I began to imitate Baldwin's style of writing, using dependent clauses whenever and wherever I could [...]. And so in my essays at school I was busy trying to cram as many commas into my sentences as I could.[61]

Indeed, as *The Price of the Ticket* unintentionally reveals, Baldwin's voice seems to have even seized possession of Maya Angelou. *I Am Not Your Negro* also reveals and calls upon the possessing power of this spirit as a guiding force in a present time of resurgent trouble. It is a warrior spirit of the streets and of the now.

Notes

1 Louis Montrose, "Professing the Renaissance: The Poetics and Politics of Culture," in *Literary Theory: An Anthology*, 2nd ed., eds. Julie Rivkin and Michael Ryan (Malden, MA: Blackwell Publishing, 2004 [1989]), 588.
2 Robert Gooding-Williams, "History of African American Political Thought and Antiracist Critical Theory," in *The Oxford Handbook of Philosophy and Race*, ed. Naomi Zack (Oxford: Oxford University Press, 2017), 236–241.

3 Edward W. Saïd, "The Politics of Knowledge," in *Falling into Theory: Conflicting Views of Reading Literature*, 2nd ed., ed. David H. Richter (Boston, MA: Bedford/St. Martin's, 2000 [1991]), 198.
4 Saïd, "The Politics of Knowledge," 199.
5 Saïd, "The Politics of Knowledge," 195.
6 Fred Hampton was executed by Chicago Police in 1969. The scene of his death was documented in footage that appears in Howard Alk's historically groundbreaking documentary, *The Murder of Fred Hampton* (1971).
7 A more in-depth discussion of the transformation of Hampton's message by Jackson can be found in Stephen Casmier, "The First Rainbow Coalition and the End of Multiculturalism in Ishmael Reed's *Mumbo Jumbo*," in *American Multiculturalism in Context: Views from at Home and Abroad*, ed. Sami Ludwig (Cambridge: Cambridge Scholars Publishing, 2017), 145–164.
8 Walter Benjamin, "Theses on the Philosophy of History," in *Illuminations: Essays and Reflections*, trans. Harry Zohn, ed. Hannah Arendt (New York: Mariner Books, 2019 [1968]), 110.
9 Karen Thorsen, *The James Baldwin Project*, http://jamesbaldwinproject.org/KTBio.html. Accessed 8 October 2019.
10 Charles Trueheart, "Powerful 'Baldwin'; PBS's Masterly Portrait of the Writer," *The Washington Post*, 14 August 1989.
11 James Campbell, "James Baldwin: The Price of the Ticket," *Monthly Film Bulletin*, 1 June 1990, 164.
12 Stephen Holden, "Gay and Lesbian Festival Widens Its Film Horizons," *The New York Times*, 31 May 1990; Stephen Holden, "The Games Begin; Things to Do With a Gay Flavor," (25th Anniversary of the Stonewall Uprising), *The New York Times*, 17 June 1994.
13 Tambay Obenson, "Hey New York! 'The Devil Finds Work: James Baldwin on Film' Series Kicks Off Tomorrow, Sept. 11," *indieWire*, 10 September 2015.
14 Henry Louis Gates, Jr., "The Fire Last Time," in *Blooms Modern Critical Views: James Baldwin*, ed. Harold Bloom (New York: Infobase Publishing, 2007 [1992]), 13.
15 Gates, "The Fire Last Time," 16.
16 Gates, "The Fire Last Time," 16.
17 Gates, "The Fire Last Time," 16.
18 Gates, "The Fire Last Time," 19.
19 Gates, "The Fire Last Time," 22.
20 Combahee River Collective, "The Combahee River Collective Statement," in *Home Girls: A Black Feminist Anthology*, ed. Barbara Smith (New Brunswick, NJ: Rutgers University Press, 2000 [1983]), 267.
21 Combahee, "The Combahee River Collective Statement," 264.
22 Thomas A. Johnson, "38 Report on Life in Black America: Hampton before Death Told Interviewers of Struggle," *New York Times Magazine*, 27 June 1971.
23 John Herbers, "Chicago's Operation Breadbasket Is Seeking Racial Solutions in Economic Problems," *New York Times Magazine*, 2 June 1963, 31.
24 Mary Louise Pratt, "Humanities for the Future: Reflections on the Western Culture Debate at Stanford," in *Falling into Theory: Conflicting Views on Reading Literature*, ed. David Richter (Boston, MA: Bedford of St. Martin's Press, 1994), 60.
25 Clyde Taylor, "Amazing Grace: Celebrating Jimmy," in *James Baldwin: The Legacy*, ed. Quincy Troupe (New York: Simon and Schuster, 1989), 36.

26 Jason Schneiderman, "I Thought I Hated Inaugural Poems (But It Turns Out I Don't)," *The American Poetry Review* 41, no. 2 (March/April 2012): 12.
27 Schneiderman, "I Thought I Hated," 12.
28 In its ranking of African American scholars according to the number of times they are mentioned in the national press, *The Journal of Blacks in Higher Education* observed that in 1999, "Professor Angelou was mentioned in newspapers and magazines far more often than any other black scholar or literary figure." "JBHE's Citation Rankings in the Social Sciences and the Humanities," *The Journal of Blacks in Higher Education*, no. 28 (Summer 2000): 16.
29 Geneva Smitherman, "The Power of the Rap: The Black Idiom and the New Black Poetry," *Twentieth Century Literature* 19, no. 4 (October 1973): 260.
30 Walter Goodman, "James Baldwin Portrait, Self- and Otherwise," *The New York Times*, 14 August 1989.
31 Douglas Field, "Looking for Jimmy Baldwin: Sex, Privacy, and Black Nationalist Fervor," *Callaloo* 27, no. 2 (Spring 2004): 457.
32 Field, "Looking for Jimmy Baldwin," 457.
33 Dwight McBride, "Introduction: 'How Much Time Do You Want for Your Progress? New Approaches to James Baldwin," in *James Baldwin Now*, ed. Dwight McBride (New York: New York University Press, 1999), 9.
34 Richard Goldstein, "Go the Way Your Blood Beats: An Interview with James Baldwin" (1984), in *James Baldwin: The Last Interview and Other Conversations* (Brooklyn: Melville House Publishing, 2014).
35 Eldridge Cleaver, *Soul on Ice* (New York: McGraw-Hill, 1968), 99.
36 Cleaver, *Soul on Ice*, 109.
37 Gates, "The Fire Last Time," 16.
38 Cleaver, *Soul on Ice*, 105.
39 Benjamin, "Theses on the Philosophy of History," 110.
40 Craig Phillips, "How 'I Am Not Your Negro' Filmmaker Reopened James Baldwin's 'House'," 10 January 2018, www.pbs.org/independentlens/blog/i-am-not-your-negro-filmmakers-reopen-james-baldwins-house/. Accessed 19 November 2019.
41 Aramide Tinubu, "Raoul Peck on His Oscar-Nominated 'I Am Not Your Negro,' Encountering James Baldwin and Confronting America," *Shadow and Act*, 20 April 2017, https://shadowandact.com/2017/02/01/interview-filmmaker-raoul-peck-on-his-oscar-nominated-i-am-not-your-negro-encountering-james-baldwin-confronting-america/. Accessed 19 November 2019.
42 Raoul Peck, *I Am Not Your Negro* (A Companion Edition to the Documentary Film Directed by Raoul Peck), (New York: Vintage International, 2017), xiv.
43 Peck, *I Am Not Your Negro*, xv.
44 Peck, *I Am Not Your Negro*, xvii.
45 Peck, *I Am Not Your Negro*, xxii.
46 Burlin Barr, "Raoul Peck's 'Lumumba' and 'Lumumba: La mort du prophète': On Cultural Amnesia and Historical Erasure," *African Studies Review* 54, no. 1 (April 2011): 94.
47 Montrose, "Professing the Renaissance," 588.
48 Peck, *I Am Not Your Negro*, xvii.

49 Peck, *I Am Not Your Negro*, xvii.
50 Maya Deren, *Divine Horsemen: The Living Gods of Haiti* (Kingston, NY: McPherson & Co, 2004 [1953]), 27.
51 Deren, *Divine Horsemen*, 28.
52 Deren, *Divine Horsemen*, 27.
53 Deren, *Divine Horsemen*, 32.
54 Deren, *Divine Horsemen*, 27.
55 Deren, *Divine Horsemen*, 29.
56 Deren, *Divine Horsemen*, 31.
57 Deren, *Divine Horsemen*, 29.
58 Deren, *Divine Horsemen*, 33.
59 Deren, *Divine Horsemen*, 29.
60 Amiri Baraka, "Jimmy!: Eulogy for James Baldwin," in *Eulogies* (New York: Marsilio Publishers, 1996), 93.
61 Gates, "The Fire Last Time," 13.

5 Techniques for truth-telling from *Haitian Corner* to *I Am Not Your Negro*

Toni Pressley-Sanon

The international filmmaker Raoul Peck is part of a long tradition of artist-activist-scholars who use their work to bear witness to and protest socio-political, economic, and intellectual injustice. This tradition of what may be simply called speaking truth to power is found in the abolitionist Frederick Douglass's 1 December 1850 speech entitled "The Nature of Slavery" in which he asserts his "right to speak and to speak *strongly*" and "truly" about his disdain for the institution of slavery.[1] We find the continuation of this compulsion to speak truly and strongly against injustice poignantly in the 20th century in the writer and critic Toni Morrison's declaration in her essay "The Site of Memory" that she feels that, as a person who is a member of two marginalized groups (Black and a woman), her "gravest responsibility…is not to lie."[2] She goes on to differentiate between "fact" and "truth," asserting that facts can exist without human intervention; truth cannot. The distinction she makes is important because it addresses the need for those who are committed to social justice to use faculties beyond the five senses to excavate those stories that are persistently erased, ignored, or suppressed in the service of white supremacy.

Douglass and Morrison exemplify what theologian and public intellectual Cornel West, in his 1993 treatise, *Race Matters*, declares is his basic aim in life: "to speak the truth to power with love so that the quality of everyday life for ordinary people is enhanced and white supremacy is stripped of its authority and legitimacy."[3] All of these leaders' declarations regarding their commitment to truth-telling is matched by their cultural and political work on behalf of the oppressed: those still held in bondage in Douglass's time and those who continue to suffer the violence of marginalization and erasure of West's and Morrison's now. Morrison has gone on to express what she sees as another of her jobs as a writer: to have her art serve a political and social good. She says, addressing the reader of her 1984 essay "Rootedness,"

> If anything I do, in the way of writing novels (or whatever I write) isn't about the village or the community or about you, then it is not about anything. I am not interested in indulging myself in some private, closed exercise of my imagination that fulfills the obligation of my personal dreams—which is to say yes, the work must be political.[4]

The writer, playwright, and critic James Arthur Baldwin, the subject of one of Peck's recent artistic endeavors, also made the commitment to fuse his art with his politics in the service of justice. Both (art and politics) were integral to his peripatetic life.[5]

As a filmmaker who describes himself as a "responsible citizen" and who likewise leads a peripatetic life, Peck also marries his art and his politics.[6] As Pascal Bonitzer, a long-time collaborator with Peck observes, political commitment permeates and informs his films, reflecting and giving voice to "the indomitable anger and irony of the oppressed."[7] This chapter explores a few of what I call truth-telling techniques that the filmmaker deploys, not only in his documentary film that centers Baldwin, *I Am Not Your Negro* (2016), but in several of his other films, all in the service of realizing universal human liberation.

Peck's devotion to speaking truth to power drives his oeuvre, evidenced in some of his earliest feature films, *Haitian Corner* (1987) and *The Man by the Shore* (1993), both about the trauma that Haitian citizens suffered under François (Papa Doc) Duvalier and then Jean-Claude (Baby Doc) Duvalier, as well as *Desounen: Dialogue with Death* (1994), a meditation on the close proximity of death with which the Haitian poor contend on a daily basis. We see it in *Profit and Nothing But! Or Impolite Thoughts on the Class Struggle* (2001), a wide view and sweeping indictment of capitalism and "globalization" and its ravages. It appears again when he returned to the feature film genre to focus on the particularity of the divisions inflicted on the colony by the metropole and that erupted in the 1994 Rwandan genocide in *Sometimes in April* (2005). His compulsion also is clear in his two films about the murder of Patrice Lumumba, the first president of the Democratic Republic of Congo: *Lumumba: Death of a Prophet (Lumumba: la mort du prophète,* 1990), a documentary, and *Lumumba* (2000), a fictional adaptation. We find it in his later feature film, *Moloch Tropical* (2009), another searing portrayal of the propensity for "absolute power to corrupt absolutely," which, as Bonitzer observes, intermingles the figures of the Duvaliers and President Jean-Bertrand Aristide under whom Peck served as Minister of Culture for 18 months, "but goes beyond them to all powers-that-be who are prey to hubris (Berlusconi, Nixon and…Clinton)."[8] Peck uses his camera, again, to shed a spotlight on sociopolitical and economic injustice in his documentary, *Fatal Assistance* (2013), released just two years following the earthquake that devastated Haiti in 2010 and his follow-up feature film *Murder in Pacot* (2014), released one year later, which plays with the class and spatial relationship of above (*anleya*) and below (*anba*) to comment on the stark societal inequity that the earthquake revealed. Peck brings many of these truth-telling techniques that he uses in his earlier films to bear in *I Am Not Your Negro*, again, in the service of social justice.[9]

The work of witnessing

In *I Am Not Your Negro*, Peck takes up the work of bearing witness, protesting injustice, and – in the tradition of his predecessors like Douglass and later, Baldwin, as well as his contemporaries, like West and Morrison – speaking truth to power, at this, again, dangerous time in American and world politics. Indeed, as Warren Crichlow observes, "Peck carries Baldwin's prescient voice into the twenty-first century where his rhetorical practice of 'telling it like it is' resonates anew in this perilous political moment."[10] One of the reasons that it resonates so strongly is that, while following Baldwin's lead, Peck demonstrates, as he has repeatedly done throughout his career, his own commitment to "telling it like it is."

Peck's commitment to truth-telling in the name of social justice is a logical outgrowth of his heritage and upbringing. As he writes in the introduction to the companion book, *I Am Not Your Negro*, about his inspiration for the film, although his country of origin fought and beat the most powerful country in the world to stop "slavery in its tracks," the revolution that produced the first Black republic in the western hemisphere has been ignored by history because it "rendered the dominant narrative of the day" – that people of African descent were destined for slavery and incapable of self-governance – "untenable."[11] He then recounts a childhood in New York where a large Oriental rug with images of the martyred leaders, John F. Kennedy and Dr. Martin Luther King, Jr., depicted as equals, hung in his family's apartment, but which he became keenly aware did not reflect social reality. Finally, his learning of the three men who were the subject of Baldwin's unfinished manuscript, "Remember This House," Medgar Evers, Malcolm X, and Martin Luther King, was the last of the catalysts for his ensuing deep and personal reflection on his "own political and cultural mythology" as well as his "own experiences of racism and intellectual violence," both of which propel his politics and his art.[12]

Invoking the cadre of pathbreakers who bring truths to light, Peck has written about his entrance into filmmaking as a process of "stealing" images that didn't – and weren't supposed to – exist.[13] His remarks evoke not only the history of the Haitian Revolution, an event that was "unthinkable" to the French colonizers, in the words of the anthropologist Michel-Rolph Trouillot,[14] but also the words of Douglass who recalls in his autobiography his master's words about the "unthinkability" of an educated slave.[15] It also recalls the words of Morrison who, in speaking about the inspiration for *The Bluest Eye* (1970), her first novel, says that she wrote it because it was a book she wanted to read and that she couldn't find anywhere.[16] Similarly, Peck produces films that, because they render "the dominant narrative untenable," would not otherwise be found anywhere.

Peck's insistence on injecting the "unthinkable" into the dominant narrative follows in the tradition of Baldwin who, in a scene from *I Am Not Your Negro*, can be seen on *The Dick Cavett Show* elucidating the American racial double standard that circumscribes Black life. In declaring that had Nat Turner been white he would have been a hero and had Malcolm X been white he would probably be alive, Baldwin prompts the audience to speculate on the fates of other potential Black revolutionaries, including perhaps those of Peck's Haiti, had they been white. Indeed, Peck's remarks regarding the fate of Haiti echo those of Baldwin regarding any African American revolutionary figure who, as Baldwin concludes, whites judge as criminal and treat him as such, with everything possible being done to make an example of the "bad nigger" so that "there won't be any more like him" (Figure 5.1).[17]

Figure 5.1 James Baldwin and Dick Cavett on *The Dick Cavett Show* in *I Am Not Your Negro* (Raoul Peck, 2016).

Peck's filmmaking process of "stealing" is something that he has done since his first feature film, *Haitian Corner*, convinced as he is that, as a person whose history and experience has been marginalized, the only reason to make films is to "keep stealing" – in other words, to think the unthinkable and imagine the unimaginable.[18] Invoking other sociopolitically driven artists, he says, "We are stealing images in the sense that we are creating images that are not supposed to be, that are not already considered legitimate, whether aesthetically, dramatically, or even economically."[19] He works from the position that the (deeply flawed) dominant narrative of Hollywood does not reflect his experience because it is exclusionary, isolating, alienating, and, most of all, simplistic. There are several ways in which Peck exposes and counters such narratives in *I Am Not Your Negro*. He does so, for example, by following a scene from John Stahl's 1934 film *Imitation of Life* in which the lie of Peola, a young girl passing for white, is exposed when her Black mother comes to school to pick her up, with the photo of the lived reality of 15-year-old Dorothy Counts enduring the abuse of whites at the school that she was tasked with integrating in North Carolina in 1957. And again, he deploys a similar strategy in preceding the violence of the 1911 photo of the lynched Laura Nelson in Oklahoma with the glittery innocence of Doris Day in the film *Lover Come Back* (Delbert Mann, 1961). In both instances, the voice-over quotation of Baldwin's oft-quoted truism, "Not everything that is faced can be changed, but nothing can be changed until it is faced" brings into stark relief the "exclusionary, isolating, alienating, and simplistic" nature of the Hollywood narratives that are produced for white America in the face of the everyday violence that African Americans endure. In order to uncover the complexity of the world excised from the "dominant narrative," he resolved to, as he says, "go behind the curtain into the kitchen,"[20] and perhaps as Audre Lorde would phrase it, use the tools of the master to dismantle his house.[21]

Drawing on Baldwin's own methodology, Peck asserts that the work of telling the stories that are left out of Hollywood meant and continues to mean using the merchandise, borrowing the cooks and helpers, and mixing the ingredients in new ways in order to "change the flavors, break some glasses and cook… a kind of pungent missionary stew – a funky dish of chitterlings."[22] In other words, as Crichlow remarks about the film, "Peck, like Baldwin, refuses in *I Am Not Your Negro* to bow down to the master texts of Western history, but rather recalibrates cinema's tools for a renewed ownership."[23] In this way, Peck is continuing the work and play of signifying for which African Americans are so well known: appropriating words and technologies that have been used against them to "flip the script" on the oppressor.

Peck includes in *I Am Not Your Negro* a voice-over of Baldwin remarking that he came to accept that, as a writer, his responsibility in the civil rights movement was to bear witness. This work of witnessing entailed moving as largely and as freely as possible to write the story and get it out. Baldwin's realization could just as easily be attributed to Peck who has used his filmmaking career to also bear witness, to get the story out. The magnitude of this responsibility becomes clear when we consider what is entailed in uncovering truth(s) and then getting them out in a world that would keep them hidden.

Peck's feature films about Haiti involved piecing together often fragmented stories of those who had suffered under the Duvaliers. This piecing together of narratives of one of the nadirs of Haitian history was necessitated by the shroud of silence that had been pulled over the myriad ways that people suffered, as well as the depth of their suffering, under the Duvalier regime. It was also necessitated by the international community's willful blindness to the human rights atrocities that were everyday occurrences in the Duvaliers' Haiti at a time when the country was receiving major American financial support. The ever-present threat of violence coupled with the reality of the number of people dead and disappeared, as well as the desire by those who had lived through it to bury the trauma, means that the work of unearthing the stories necessary to create a holistic picture of life and death under the Duvaliers is daunting. The fragmented stories that Peck was able to collect have formed the basis of several of his films, beginning with *Haitian Corner*, about a young man living in Brooklyn who is haunted by his memories of his torture by the *Tonton Macoutes*, the Duvaliers' paramilitary force, years before. As Peck writes about his conceptualization of *Haitian Corner*, he was inspired by two women, Denise Prophete and Laurette Badette, both of whom had spent eight years in Fort Dimanche, the Duvaliers' prison from which prisoners were meant to never emerge alive, and who gave him the "film's soul."[24] Although neither of the women appear in the film, inspired by their stories, he begins *Haitian Corner* with testimonies from a sampling of "real"[25] victims who bear witness to the suffering of thousands.

This witnessing returns in several of his other films in different forms. In commenting on the form that it takes in *I Am Not Your Negro*, Crichlow remarks, "viewers become spellbound by this critical witness's fervent idiomatic eloquence and uncompromising vision."[26] It is worth noting that Crichlow's referent for the "critical witness" is ambivalent. The reader is not sure whether he is referring to Baldwin, to Peck, or to the film itself. He could be referring to all three simultaneously as, in the unfinished manuscript that inspired *I Am Not Your Negro*, Baldwin was committed to the work of bearing witness on behalf of his three friends, Malcolm, Martin, and Medgar, all fierce warriors for justice who had been murdered at the height of the civil rights era when the lie of American equality and democracy was unraveling internationally. Because Peck has long committed his life to bearing witness to the injustice that he has seen on an international front, *I Am Not Your Negro* may be viewed then, ultimately, as bearing witness to Peck's bearing witness to Baldwin's bearing witness – a kind of triple witnessing that is inextricable from the subject and his posthumous collaborator.

Peck has discussed the challenge of bearing witness to realities shrouded in silence in not only Haiti but also the Congo. For example, when he began conceptualizing his biopic about Patrice Lumumba, Peck was faced with structuring the work "around the fissures that made Lumumba's story impossible to tell or to resolve via closure" precisely because it is impossible to fully know.[27] Peck's desire to tell the story of Lumumba's death was also haunted by the propaganda that surrounded the revolutionary figure. To help suture some of those fissures, in *Lumumba: Death of a Prophet*, Peck relies on the stories his mother used to tell him to frame the biopic, thus allowing him to tell history in a way that challenges the dominant narrative about the public figure who had been maligned in popular media. As Peck writes about the challenge of conceptualizing the film, he had to unlearn everything he had learned about Lumumba, describing it as a deeply painful process. I quote Peck at length here because it speaks to the challenges that the marginalized and silenced have had to face historically and continue to face as they go about the work of truth-telling in the service of a liberated humanity:

> First of all, it took me a year and a half before I could begin to accept Lumumba as a sympathetic character. I couldn't warm up to him, and the reasons for my alienation eluded me. Then I realized that everything I had learned about Lumumba came from the same sources—journalists or politicians from the West who had covered the crisis in the Congo. For them, it was a fearful, traumatic, and arrogant confrontation and they had responded by investing their understanding of Lumumba with all the usual, racist, clichés. I had been contaminated by those clichés. The underlying racism of the world's biggest newspapers, of the *New York Times*, or *Le Monde*, was naïve in a way. It represented how the world saw Africa, not in political terms, but in primitive, one-dimensional, tribalistic terms.[28]

Indeed, as Peck observes, while politics in European nations are recognized as complex and multilayered, this is not the case when it comes to Africa. As a result of the simplistic, racist portrayals of Lumumba that he had consumed until that point, he began his project with the perception of his subject as a "crazy, uneducated, ambitious, and corrupt leader."[29] The process of unlearning and then relearning about Lumumba with the goal of truth-telling taught him "the importance and challenge of shaping one's image."[30] In *Stolen Images*, in which he discusses his process of unlearning the falsehoods perpetuated by those who have the power to shape so many narratives, he adds a directive to the reader: "You must hold the key to your own image-making because if you don't, other people will. And this is the real problem of storytelling: who controls your image, who tells your story."[31]

Peck's directive – an underlying principle in all of his works – also drove Baldwin's life and work. It may be seen as the reason that, while writing and publishing steadily and producing an impressive amount of fiction and nonfiction, Baldwin also maintained a robust public intellectual and activist life. He was constantly working to control his image apart from and beyond the labels that a society that did not love him constantly tried to impose upon him (i.e. "nigger," "negro writer").[32] Although Baldwin was very much a public figure and the kinds of silences that characterize the subject of several of Peck's previous films are not present, Peck, nonetheless, faced the daunting task of again locating presences in the absences when he began working on *I Am Not Your Negro*. In his reflections about the process of composing the film, Peck remarks that the "manuscript" which Baldwin envisioned would become "Remember This House" was a "self-reflexive reexamination of recent American experience" through the lives of his friends who had been murdered in rapid succession.[33] The zygote of a narrative that Baldwin left behind "offered a portal through which to conceptualize the film."[34] Turning those pages into a film entailed finding the "'unwritten book' to use as a device for creating a dramatic structure that could help make the film speak with striking truth-telling relevance."[35]

Peck's building on Baldwin's narrative reflects not only his commitment to bearing witness but also a deep and sustained commitment to inserting the unthinkable into the dominant narrative. Thus, when Morrison argues that the job of the artist who is a member of a group whose stories have been silenced by History is to "rip that veil drawn over proceedings too terrible to relate," we must beg the question, too terrible for whom? Baldwin's, and I would add Peck's, answer is those who were able to maintain their "innocence" while profiting from the systems that were built to shield them from the lived experience of the exploited and oppressed.[36] Peck takes up Morrison's call to relate those proceedings "too terrible to relate" in the name of not only African diasporic liberation, something to which Baldwin was also committed, but also white liberation, as part and parcel of his demonstrated commitment to, ultimately, the achievement of global liberation.

Techniques of truth-telling

Peck deploys several filmic techniques to bear witness in his films. These include establishing complementary and oppositional relationships as well as using voice-over, montage, and *tableau vivant* to connect the story of one with that of the many, the past to the present, above to below. We see his attention to dialectical and dyadic relationships in several of his films, for example, in his use of the Citadel Laferriere, built during the reign of King Henri Christophe in the first years of Haiti's independence as the setting for his dramatization of contemporary global examples of despots in *Moloch Tropical*. It is found as well in the conflict between brothers in *Sometimes in April* and in the dyadic relationship that he plays with between above and below in *Murder in Pacot*. We also see it in his conceptualization of *I Am Not Your Negro* through the parallels that he draws between images, both still and moving, of victimized African Americans and the subsequent protests that turned them into household names. The lives and deaths of these "ordinary" victims are inextricable from the lives and deaths of Baldwin's three famous friends, but with a difference. While the lives and deaths of the many "ordinary" victims of racist violence have been politicized after the fact, Baldwin's friends' lives and deaths are framed by political upheaval. The social injustice the men witnessed and suffered propelled them into the spotlight and made them targets for assassination. As such, their murders were inherently political. But while it may seem at first glance that the other victims of racist violence that Peck features in the film are not political, his pairing their stories with those of Baldwin's friends demands that the audience recognize the inherent politicization of Black life and death. Hence, Peck visually reinforces the narrative thread of *I Am Not Your Negro* that connects the fate of one with that of the many, of those above with those below, and the past with the present – something to which Baldwin was also committed.

Peck realizes Baldwin's commitment and vision right from the outset by opening the film with the author's 1968 interview with Cavett in which Baldwin states that the real question to ask is not about the "fate of the Negro" but about "what is going to happen to this country," immediately followed by contemporary scenes of African American protestors facing off against majority white police officers dressed in riot gear while a blues song pulls the scenes together. The narrative thread that connects the one with the many returns later in the voice-over of Baldwin declaring wearily, "The story of the Negro in America is the story of America. It is not a pretty story." Such scenes, complemented by voice-over and sprinkled throughout the film, stay true not only to Baldwin's desire to "tell the story of America through the lives of three of his murdered friends" but also to Peck's desire to contribute to a socially just world using his art.

Peck has long used voice-over to support and augment his visual imagery. For example, the voice-over in his biopic *Lumumba: Death of a Prophet* invests his mother with the authority for the history that he tells. In his documentary *Profit and Nothing But!* the voice-over acts as a guide through visual images of the devastating effects of rampant capitalist consumption and globalization on the poor. In his feature film, *The Man by the Shore*, the voice-over of an adult Sarah, the protagonist – recalling the words of her disappeared grandmother soothing her when she was a child after she witnessed her uncle's torture at the hands of a Macoute – speaks to the lasting trauma of the dictatorship. We also find this use of the voice-over in *Desounen: Dialogue with Death*, presented as an ongoing conversation between a Haitian peasant and Death that frames the interviews and scenes from peasant life that constitute the majority of the film and provides a narrative thread to guide the viewer through the disparate, yet interwoven stories. The voice-over by Samuel L. Jackson in *I Am Not Your Negro* is a brilliant continuation of Peck's technique, which as Crichlow rightly observes "insinuates rather than replicates, creating a parallel universe to Baldwin's inimitable lyrical presence" with Jackson channeling "the radical power of [Baldwin's] declamatory speech."[37]

Two final related techniques Peck uses to bear witness in *I Am Not Your Negro* – montage and *tableau vivant* – can also be found in several of his other films. For example, a variation of the montage featuring different representations of Black humanity toward the end of the film is found in *Haitian Corner* in the testimonies of three victims of the Duvalier regime. Similarly, in *Desounen*, the montage of testimonials comes shortly after the framing conversation between the peasant and Death has begun and is preceded by a momentary scene of the ocean while the voice-over of the peasant tells Death that before he embarks on his final journey, he needs "to record the testimony of the living."[38] The testimonials are, like that in *Haitian Corner*, first delivered by a woman and then by two men. However, unlike that in *Haitian Corner*, the testimonies are delivered outside, with a stone wall behind the testifiers and sounds of what the viewer can assume is daily life in Haiti in the background.

All of the testifiers in *Desounen* are well dressed and look to be middle-class professionals. And while they use French, the language of the upper class, to acknowledge their own privilege, they also acknowledge the reality of the poor and marginalized: those who perhaps suffered the torture that the victims from *Haitian Corner* suffered and who feel compelled to take to the ocean in unseaworthy vessels. Toward the end of *Desounen*, after so much loss has been presented, the viewer is offered a glimpse of hope: another montage featuring school children who, speaking both French and Kreyòl, tell of wanting to be journalists, nurses, and lawyers as sounds of other children playing in the background can be heard. While in the opening sequence the viewer can identify with those who have lived and seen suffering, similar to the way the audience can see their own child in the little girl and grandmother of *The Man by the Shore*, in the final scenes of *Desounen*, viewers may be able to see their own children in those who tell of their hopes and dreams for the future. Though produced 25 years after *Desounen*, the *tableau vivant* at the end of *I Am Not Your Negro* also asks the viewer to recognize themselves and their loved ones in those featured. The stone wall that serves as the background for the *tableau vivant* at the beginning of *Desounen* and later in *I Am Not Your Negro* reinforces the call to recognition in its drawing a visual connection across films and geographical boundaries as well as time and space (Figure 5.2).

Figure 5.2 Tableau of men and women of African descent in *I Am Not Your Negro* (Raoul Peck, 2016).

Coming on the heels as it does of, as Crichlow describes it,

> black and white archival footage of civil rights-era violence and recent news depicting urban rebellions in response to numerous killings of young African American citizens—from Ferguson's Michael Brown to North Carolina's Walter Scott to Baltimore's Freddie Gray to Chicago's Aiyana Mo'Nay Stanley Jones (seven years old) to Cleveland's twelve-year-old Tamir Rice to the hundreds of other lives extinguished by law 'enforcers' under bewildering circumstances since 1999,

the tableau draws almost a direct line between the violence that people of African descent suffered in the past and today.[39] The series of "archival black-and-white photographs of self-respecting black tradesmen, bright-eyed school children, and dignified society-types posed in formal attire" recall those featured at the beginning and end of *Desounen* as well as the "colored tableau of well-appointed contemporary black women and men who hold the viewer's gaze in a succession of tightly cropped shots" to a similar effect, of depicting the humanity of those who are othered by those who, under the delusion of white supremacy, dehumanize, vilify, and murder them.[40] Thus, we can see that in *I Am Not Your Negro*, Peck's commitment to social justice is again evidenced by the connections that he insists upon making across time and space. Like his other films, this film works in direct opposition to a global ideology based on exploitative violence that is dependent on our collective apathy and amnesia, reflecting Peck's commitment to sincerely and truthfully stating "his political and humanist struggles."[41] In other words, he tells it like it is.

As Crichlow maintains, James Baldwin was and continues to be significant to ongoing African American claims on human rights. But he is also significant to the universal struggle for emancipation of all human beings. Peck, in bringing his vision for Baldwin's words to the screen as one of the latest additions to his oeuvre, has yet again demonstrated his own significance to the fates of African and African diasporic claims to human rights and to the continuing struggle to demonstrate how they are inextricable from universal human rights. He uses his art to speak truth to power in the service of dismantling the white supremacist structures that make the past very much present as well as prescient in this time of reinvigorated racism, classism, xenophobia, homophobia, and sexism on a global scale. It also, like several of Peck's other films, bears witness to both the present and the future: his "sole goal."[42]

Like Baldwin, Peck rejects labels that others would foist upon him – in his case, a politically committed, *engagé* filmmaker. Rather, he describes himself as a "responsible citizen" who offers words and another viewpoint to people watching his movies, hopefully enabling them to see the world they belong to in different ways.[43] And like Baldwin's writings, the films that Peck unflinchingly imagines into existence allow him to leave a mark and contribute to the centering of stories that need to be told for the power they hold to liberate all of us.

Notes

1. Frederick Douglass, "The Nature of Slavery," in *African Philosophy: An Anthology*, ed. Emmanuel Chukwudi Eze (Malden, MA: Blackwell Publishing, 1998), 375.
2. Toni Morrison, "The Site of Memory," in *Inventing the Truth: The Art and Craft of Memoir*, ed. William Zinser (Boston, MA: Houghton Mifflin, 1995), 93.
3. Cornel West, *Race Matters* (Boston, MA: Beacon Press, 1993), x.
4. Toni Morrison, "Rootedness: The Ancestor as Foundation," in *Black Women Writers (1950–1980): A Critical Evaluation*, ed. Mari Evans (New York: Anchor Books, 1984), 344.
5. Warren Crichlow, "Baldwin's Rendezvous with the Twenty-First Century: *I Am Not Your Negro*," *Film Quarterly* 7, no. 4 (Summer 2017): 10.
6. "Biography," *Raoul Peck: 6 Films* (Paris, France: Institut Français, 2013), n.p.
7. Pascal Bonitzer, "Raoul Peck a Long Story," in *Raoul Peck: 6 Films* (Paris, France: Institut Francais, 2013), n.p.
8. Bonitzer, "Raoul Peck a Long Story," n.p.
9. Peck's biopic, *Le jeune Karl Marx* (The Young Karl Marx, 2017), about the socialist revolutionary, also uses several of these truth-telling techniques that Peck deploys in those earlier films, including *I Am Not Your Negro*.
10. Crichlow, "Baldwin's Rendezvous," 9.
11. Raoul Peck, "Introduction: On a Personal Note," in *I Am Not Your Negro: A Companion Edition to the Documentary Film Directed by Raoul Peck from Texts by James Baldwin* (New York: Vintage International, 2017), ix.
12. Peck, "Introduction: On a Personal Note," xi.
13. Raoul Peck, *Stolen Images* (New York: Seven Stories Press, 2012), 13.
14. Michel-Rolph Trouillot, *Silencing the Past: Power and the Production of History* (Boston, MA: Beacon Press, 1995).
15. Frederick Douglass, *Narrative of the Life of Frederick Douglass* (New York: Dover Publications, Inc., 1995), 20.
16. "'Why I Wrote *The Bluest Eye*,' An Interview with Toni Morrison," www.youtube.com/watch?v=I0JkI3F6z-Y.
17. Baldwin speaking with Dick Cavett in *I Am Not Your Negro*.
18. Peck, *Stolen Images*, 13.
19. Peck, *Stolen Images*, 13–14.
20. Peck, *Stolen Images*, 14.

21 Lorde argues against this possibility in her essay "The Master's Tools Will Never Dismantle the Master's House" in relation to exclusionary white feminist heteronormative and classist politics. However, what we see with Baldwin and now with Peck is a reimagining of those tools that have been traditionally used against the marginalized and oppressed to inject themselves into narratives that attempt to silence and erase them.
22 Peck, *Stolen Images*, 14.
23 Crichlow, "Baldwin's Rendezvous," 12.
24 Peck, *Stolen Images*, 15.
25 I put "real" in quotations because it is unclear whether those featured in the film as testifiers are actors or actual victims of the Tonton Macoutes.
26 Crichlow, "Baldwin's Rendezvous," 9.
27 Crichlow, "Baldwin's Rendezvous," 13–14.
28 Peck, *Stolen Images*, 113.
29 Peck, *Stolen Images*, 113.
30 Peck, *Stolen Images*, 113.
31 Peck, *Stolen Images*, 113.
32 I am alluding here to Baby Sugg's open-air sermon from Toni Morrison's *Beloved* in which she encourages her congregation to love themselves for "they" do not love them. Toni Morrison, *Beloved* (New York: Penguin Group, 1987).
33 Crichlow, "Baldwin's Rendezvous," 9.
34 Crichlow, "Baldwin's Rendezvous," 9.
35 Crichlow, "Baldwin's Rendezvous," 9.
36 I am referring here to Baldwin's declaration in *The Fire Next Time*: "But it is not permissible that the authors of devastation should also be innocent. It is the innocence which constitutes the crime" (5–6).
37 Crichlow, "Baldwin's Rendezvous," 14. Most recently, he has used the voice-over technique effectively at the end of *The Young Karl Marx* in which the actor, August Diehl, can be heard reading critical passages from Marx's unfinished masterpiece, *The Communist Manifesto*, while a *tableau vivant* of the poor and disenfranchised occupy the screen. These scenes, shot in black and white, and resembling archival footage, are followed by powerful shots in both black and white and in color, of capitalist production and juxtaposed with scenes of rebellion and political leaders from Castro to Reagan, from Thatcher to Lumumba to Mandela, and interposed with scenes of contemporary disenfranchisement of the marginalized poor.
38 The ocean represents both salvation and death for the millions who attempt the voyage to other lands to escape the crushing poverty and political repression of their native land.
39 Crichlow, "Baldwin's Rendezvous," 12.
40 Crichlow, "Baldwin's Rendezvous," 12.
41 "Biography," *Raoul Peck: 6 Films* (Paris, France: Institut Francais, 2013), n.p.
42 "Haitian Corner," *Raoul Peck: 6 Films* (Paris, France: Institut Francais, 2013), n.p.
43 "Biography," *Raoul Peck: 6 Films*, n.p.

Bibliography

Baldwin, James. *The Devil Finds Work* (1976). New York: Vintage, 2013.
———. *The Fire Next Time* (1963). New York: Vintage International, 1993.
———. "The Harlem Ghetto" (1948). In *Notes of a Native Son*, 51–64. Boston, MA: Beacon Press, 1984.
———. *No Name in the Street* (1972). New York: Vintage, 2013.
———. "An Open Letter to My Sister, Miss Angela Davis." *The New York Review of Books*, 7 January 1971.
———. "Sidney Poitier (1968)." In *The Cross of Redemption: Uncollected Writings*, edited by Randall Kenan, 222–230. New York: Vintage, 2011.
———. "Sweet Lorraine." *Esquire*, 1 November 1969, 139–140.
Baraka, Amiri. *Eulogies*. New York: Marsilio Publishers, 1996.
Barr, Burlin. "Raoul Peck's 'Lumumba' and "Lumumba: La mort du prophète": On Cultural Amnesia and Historical Erasure." *African Studies Review* 54, no. 1 (April 2011): 85–116.
Barthes, Roland. "The Grain of the Voice." In *Image, Music, Text*, translated by Stephen Heath, 179–189. New York: Hill and Wang, 1977.
———. *Mythologies*. Translated by Annette Lavers. New York: Hill & Wang, 1972.
———. *Roland Barthes by Roland Barthes*. Translated by Richard Howard. London: Macmillan, 1977.
———. *S/Z: An Essay*. Translated by Richard Miller. New York: Hill and Wang, 1974.
Benjamin, Walter. "Theses on the Philosophy of History." In *Illuminations: Essays and Reflections*, edited by Hannah Arendt and translated by Harry Zohn, 196–209. (1968). Boston, MA: Mariner Books, 2019.
Bonitzer, Pascal. "Raoul Peck a Long Story." In *Raoul Peck: 6 Films*. Paris, France: Institut Francais, 2013.
Boyd, Herb. "*I Am Not Your Negro*." *Cineaste* 42, no. 2 (Spring 2017): 47–49.
Brim, Matt. *James Baldwin and the Queer Imagination*. Ann Arbor: The University of Michigan Press, 2017.
Campbell, James. "James Baldwin: The Price of the Ticket." *Monthly Film Bulletin*, 1 June 1990.
Carruthers, Lee. "M. Bazin et le temps: Reclaiming the Timeliness of Cinematic Time." *Screen* 52, no. 1 (Spring 2011): 13–29.

Casmier, Stephen. "The First Rainbow Coalition and the End of Multiculturalism in Ishmael Reed's *Mumbo Jumbo*." In *American Multiculturalism in Context*, edited by Sami Ludwig, 145–164. Cambridge: Cambridge Scholars Publishing, 2017.

Chan, Andrew. "The Great Divide." *Film Comment* 53, no. 1 (January/February 2017): 54–59.

Chion, Michel. *Audio-Vision: Sound on Screen*. New York: Columbia University Press, 2019.

Cleaver, Eldridge. *Soul on Ice*. New York: McGraw-Hill, 1968.

Cobb, Michael L. "Pulpitic Publicity: James Baldwin and the Queer Uses of Religious Words." *GLQ: A Journal of Lesbian and Gay Studies* 7, no. 2 (2001): 285–312.

Collier-Thomas, Bettye and V.P. Franklin. *Sisters in the Struggle: African American Women in the Civil Rights-Black Power Movement*. New York: New York University Press, 2001.

Collins, Kathleen. "'A Place in Time' and 'Killer of Sheep': Two Radical Definitions of Adventure minus Women." In *In Color: 60 Years of Images of Minority Women in Film...1921–1981*, edited by Pearl Bowser, 5–7. New York: Third World Newsreel, 1981.

Combahee River Collective. "The Combahee River Collective Statement." *Home Girls: A Black Feminist Anthology*, edited by Barbara Smith, 264–273. New Brunswick: Rutgers University Press, 2000.

Corber, Robert J. "Queering *I Am Not Your Negro*: Or Why We Need James Baldwin More than Ever." *James Baldwin Review* 3, no. 1 (2017): 160–172.

Corrigan, Timothy. *The Essay Film: From Montaigne, after Marker*. Oxford: Oxford University Press, 2011.

Crichlow, Warren. "Baldwin's Rendezvous with the Twenty-First Century: *I Am Not Your Negro*." *Film Quarterly* 70, no. 4 (Summer 2017): 9–22.

Deren, Maya. *Divine Horsemen: The Living Gods of Haiti*. Kingston, NY: McPherson & Co, 2004.

Di Pietrantonio, Giacinto. "Fabio Mauri: No era nuevo." Fundación PROA Buenos Aires, 2014, http://proa.org/esp/exhibition-fabio-mauri.php.

Di Stefano, John. "Picturing Pasolini: Notes from a Filmmaker's Scrapbook." *Art Journal* 56, no. 2 (1997): 18–23.

Douglass, Frederick. "The Nature of Slavery." In *African Philosophy: An Anthology*, edited by Emmanuel Chukwudi Eze, 375–378. Malden, MA: Blackwell Publishing, 1998.

———. *Narrative of the Life of Frederick Douglass*. New York: Dover Publications, Inc., 1995.

Fanon, Frantz. *Black Skin, White Masks*. Translated by Richard Philcox. New York: Grove Press, 2008.

Farley, Christopher John. "*I Am Not Your Negro* Gives Fresh Voice to James Baldwin." *Wall Street Journal*, 25 January 2017, www.wsj.com/articles/i-am-not-your-negro-gives-fresh-voice-to-james-baldwin-1485354481.

Farmer, Paul. "Anthropology of Structural Violence." *Current Anthropology* 45, no. 3 (June 2004): 305–325.

Faulkner, William. *Requiem for a Nun*. New York: Vintage, 2011.

Field, Douglas. "Looking for Jimmy Baldwin: Sex, Privacy, and Black Nationalist Fervor." *Callaloo* 27, no. 2 (Spring 2004): 457–480.

Field, Douglas. "Pentecostalism and All that Jazz: Tracing James Baldwin's Religion." *Literature and Theology* 22, no. 4 (2008): 436–457.

Flaherty, Colleen. "Too Taboo for Class?" *Inside Higher Education*, 1 February 2019, www.insidehighered.com/news/2019/02/01/professor-suspended-using-n-word-class-discussion-language-james-baldwin-essay.

Foucault, Michel. "History, Discourse and Discontinuity." In *Foucault Live: (Interviews, 1961–1984)*, edited by Sylvère Lotringer and translated by Lysa Hochroth and John Johnston, 33–50. New York: Semiotext(e), 1996.

"The Games Begin; Things to Do With a Gay Flavor." (25th Anniversary of the Stonewall Uprising). *The New York Times*, 17 June 1994.

Gates, Henry Louis, Jr. "The Fire Last Time." In *Blooms Modern Critical Views: James Baldwin*, edited by Harold Bloom, 11–22. New York: Infobase Publishing, 2007.

Goldstein, Richard. "'Go the Way Your Blood Beats': An Interview with James Baldwin." In *James Baldwin: The Legacy*, edited by Quincy Troupe, 173–185. New York: Simon and Schuster, 1989.

Gooding-Williams, Robert. "History of African American Political Thought and Antiracist Critical Theory." In *The Oxford Handbook of Philosophy and Race*, edited by Naomi Zack, 235–246. New York: Oxford University Press, 2017.

Gordon, Robert. *Pasolini: Forms of Subjectivity*. Oxford: Clarendon Press, 1996.

Hartman, Saidiya. *Scenes of Subjection: Terror, Slavery, and Self-Making in Nineteenth-Century America*. Oxford: Oxford University Press, 1997.

Herbers, John. "Chicago's Operation Breadbasket Is Seeking Racial Solutions in Economic Problems." *New York Times Magazine*, 2 June 1969, 31.

Holden, Stephen. "Gay and Lesbian Festival Widens Its Film Horizons." *The New York Times*, 31 May 1990.

James, C.L.R. *The Black Jacobins: Toussaint l'Ouverture and the San Domingo Revolution*. New York: Vintage, 1989.

"JBHE's Citation Rankings in the Social Sciences and the Humanities." *The Journal of Blacks in Higher Education*, no. 28 (Summer 2000): 16–18.

Johnson, Thomas A. "Report on Life in Black America: Hampton before Death Told Interviewers of Struggle." *New York Times Magazine*, 27 June 1971, 75U.

Joyrich, Lynne. "American Dreams and Demons." *Black Scholar* 48, no. 1 (2018): 31–42.

Kaplan, Cora and Bill Schwarz. "Introduction: America and Beyond." In *James Baldwin: America and Beyond*, edited by Kaplan and Schwarz, 1–32. Ann Arbor: The University of Michigan Press, 2011.

Keeling, Kara. *Queer Times, Black Futures*. New York: New York University Press, 2019.

Kennedy, Randall. "How a Dispute Over the N-Word Became a Dispiriting Farce." *The Chronicle of Higher Education*, 8 February 2019, www.chronicle.com/article/How-a-Dispute-Over-the-N-Word/245655.

Kohn, Eric. "*I Am Not Your Negro* Review: Samuel L. Jackson Brings James Baldwin to Life in the Year's Most Important Oscar Nominee." *IndieWire*, 2 February 2017, www.indiewire.com/2017/02/i-am-not-your-negro-review-james-baldwin-raoul-peck-oscar-1201777014/.

Kristeva, Julia. *Revolution in Poetic Language*. Translated by Margaret Waller. New York: Columbia University Press, 1985.

Lipsitz, George. *Ivory Perry: A Life in the Struggle*. Philadelphia, PA: Temple University Press, 2011.

Lorde, Audre. "The Master's Tools Will Never Dismantle the Master's House." In *Sister Outsider,* 110–113. New York: Quality Paperback Book Club, 1993.

Lubiano, Waneemah. "But Compared to What?: Reading Realism, Representation, and Essentialism in *School Daze, Do the Right Thing*, and the Spike Lee Discourse." *Black American Literature Forum* 25, no. 2, Black Film Issue (Summer 1991): 253–282.

Lucca, Violet. "*I Am Not Your Negro* Review: Race, Rage and the American Dream." *Sight and Sound* 27, no. 5 (May 2017). www.bfi.org.uk/news-opinion/sight-sound-magazine/reviews-recommendations/i-am-not-your-negro-raoul-peck-race-rage-american-dream.

Mackey, Nathaniel. *Bedouin Hornbook*. Lexington: University of Kentucky, 1986.

MacKinnon, Kenneth and Michel Fabre, eds., *Conversations with Richard Wright*. Jackson: University of Mississippi Press, 1993.

McBride, Dwight, ed., *James Baldwin Now*. New York: New York University Press, 1999.

Montrose, Louis. "Professing the Renaissance: The Poetics and Politics of Culture." *Literary Theory: An Anthology*, 2nd ed., edited by Julie Rivkin and Michael Ryan, 584–591. Malden, MA: Blackwell Publishing, 2004.

Morrison, Toni. *Beloved*. New York: Penguin Group, 1987.

———. "Rootedness: The Ancestor as Foundation." In *Black Women Writers (1950–1980): A Critical Evaluation*, edited by Mari Evans, 339–345. New York: Anchor Books, 1984.

———. "The Site of Memory." In *Inventing the Truth: The Art and Craft of Memoir*, edited by William Zinser, 83–102. Boston, MA: Houghton Mifflin, 1995.

Moten, Fred. *In the Break: The Aesthetics of the Black Radical Tradition*. Minneapolis: University of Minnesota Press, 2003.

———. *Black and Blur*. Durham, NC and London: Duke University Press, 2017.

Muñoz, José. *Cruising Utopia: The Then and There of Queer Futurity*. New York: New York University Press, 2009.

Nancy, Jean-Luc. *Noli Me Tangere: On the Raising of the Body*. Translated by Sarah Clift, Pascale-Anne Brault, and Michael Naas. New York: Fordham University Press, 2008.

Obenson, Tambay. "Hey New York! 'The Devil Finds Work: James Baldwin on Film' Series Kicks Off Tomorrow, Sept. 11." *IndieWire*, 10 September 2015.

Pasolini, Pier Paolo. "La crocifissione" (1948–1949). In *Tutte le poesie*, edited by Walter Siti, vol. 1., 467–468. Milan: Mondadori, 2003.

Pasolini, Pier Paolo, and Oswald Stack. *Pasolini on Pasolini: Interviews with Oswald Stack*. London: Thames and Hudson, 1969.

Peck, Raoul. *I Am Not Your Negro* (A Companion Edition to the Documentary Film Directed by Raoul Peck). New York: Vintage International, 2017.

———. *Stolen Images*. New York: Seven Stories Press, 2012.

Phillips, Craig Phillips. "How 'I Am Not Your Negro' Filmmaker Reopened James Baldwin's 'House'." *PBS Independent Lens*, 10 January 2018, www.pbs.org/independentlens/blog/i-am-not-your-negro-filmmakers-reopen-james-baldwins-house/.

Pratt, Mary Louise. "Humanities for the Future: Reflections on the Western Culture Debate at Stanford." In *Falling into Theory: Conflicting Views on Reading Literature*, edited by David Richter, 54–63. Boston, MA: Bedford of St. Martin's Press, 1994.

Ransby, Barbara. *Ella Baker and the Black Freedom Movement: A Radical Democratic Vision*. Chapel Hill: University of North Carolina Press, 2003.

Saïd, Edward W. "The Politics of Knowledge." In *Falling into Theory: Conflicting Views of Reading Literature*, 2nd ed., edited by David H. Richter, 189–198. New York: Bedford/St. Martin's, 2000.

Schneiderman, Jason. "I Thought I Hated Inaugural Poems (But It Turns Out I Don't)." *The American Poetry Review* 41, no. 2 (March/April 2012): 11–15.

Scott, A.O. "'I Am Not Your Negro' Will Make You Rethink Race." *The New York Times*, 2 February 2017, C1.

Sedgwick, Eve Kosofsky. *Epistemology of the Closet*. Berkeley: University of California Press, 2008.

Sharpe, Christina. *In the Wake: On Blackness and Being*. Durham, NC: UNC Press, 2016.

Sinykin, Dan. "The Apocalyptic Baldwin." *Dissent* 64, no. 3 (Summer 2017): 15–19.

Smitherman, Geneva. "The Power of the Rap: The Black Idiom and the New Black Poetry." *Twentieth Century Literature* 19, no. 4 (October 1973): 259–274.

Stanley, Fred and Louis H. Pratt, eds., *Conversations with James Baldwin*. Jackson: University of Press of Mississippi, 1989.

Strauss, Alexandra. "Editing *I Am Not Your Negro*." In *I Am Not Your Negro*, edited by Raoul Peck, xix–xxi. London: Penguin, 2017.

Take This Hammer. KQED Film Unit, Directed by Richard O. Moore, San Francisco, Spring 1963.

Taylor, Clyde. "Autopsy of Terror." *Transition: An International Review* 69, no. 1 (1996): 236–246.

———. "Amazing Grace: Celebrating Jimmy." In *James Baldwin: The Legacy*, edited by Quincy Troupe, 29–37. New York: Simon and Schuster, 1989.

Tinubu, Aramide. "Raoul Peck on His Oscar-Nominated 'I Am Not Your Negro,' Encountering James Baldwin and Confronting America." *Shadow and Act*, 20 April 2017, https://shadowandact.com/2017/02/01/interview-filmmaker-raoul-peck-on-his-oscar-nominated-i-am-not-your-negro-encountering-james-baldwin-confronting-america/.

Trouillot, Michel-Rolph. *Silencing the Past: Power and the Production of History*. Boston, MA: Beacon Press, 1995.

Trueheart, Charles. "Powerful 'Baldwin'; PBS's Masterly Portrait of the Writer." *The Washington Post*, 14 August 1989.

West, Cornel. *Race Matters*. Boston, MA: Beacon Press, 1993.

"'Why I Wrote *The Bluest Eye*,' An Interview with Toni Morrison." Uploaded 8 August 2019, www.youtube.com/watch?v=I0JkI3F6z-Y.

Woubshet, Dagmawi. "The Imperfect Power of *I Am Not Your Negro*." *The Atlantic*, 8 February 2017, www.theatlantic.com/entertainment/archive/2017/02/i-am-not-your-negro-review/515976/.

Filmography

The Aggressives (Daniel Peddle, 2005)
The Cry of Jazz (Edward Bland, 1959)
The Defiant Ones (Stanley Kramer, 1968)
Desounen: Dialogue with Death (Raoul Peck, 1994)
The Dick Cavett Show (ABC, 1968–1975)
Elephant (Gus Van Sant, 2003)
Fatal Assistance (Raoul Peck, 2013)
The Gospel According to St. Matthew (*Il Vangelo secondo Matteo*, Pier Paolo Pasolini, 1964)
Guess Who's Coming to Dinner (Stanley Kramer, 1967)
Haitian Corner (Raoul Peck, 1987)
Histoire(s) du cinéma (Jean-Luc Godard, 1989–1999)
The House on Coco Road (Damani Baker, 2016)
I Am Not Your Negro (Raoul Peck, 2016)
If Beale Street Could Talk (Barry Jenkins, 2018)
Imitation of Life (John Stahl, 1934)
In the Heat of the Night (Norman Jewison, 1967)
James Baldwin: The Price of the Ticket (Karen Thorsen, 1989)
Looking for Langston (Isaac Julien, 1988)
Lorraine Hansberry: Sighted Eyes/Feeling Heart (Tracey Heather Strain, 2017)
Lover Come Back (Delbert Mann, 1961)
Lumumba: Death of Prophet (*La mort du prophète,* Raoul Peck, 1990)
Lumumba (Raoul Peck, 2000)
The Man by the Shore (Raoul Peck, 1993)
Moloch Tropical (Raoul Peck, 2009)
Murder in Pacot (Raoul Peck, 2014)
OJ: Made in America (Ezra Edelman and Caroline Waterlow, 2016)
An Oversimplification of Her Beauty (Terrance Nance, 2012)
The Pajama Game (George Abbott and Stanley Donen, 1957)
Profit and Nothing But! Or Impolite Thoughts on the Class Struggle (Raoul Peck, 2001)
Random Acts of Flyness (Terrance Nance, HBO, 2018–present)

She's Gotta Have It (Spike Lee, 1986)
Sometimes in April (Raoul Peck, 2005)
Strong Island (Yance Ford, 2017)
Take This Hammer (Richard O. Moore, 1963)
Whose Streets? (Sabaah Folayan and Damon Davis, 2017)

Contributor biographies

Courtney R. Baker is Associate Professor in the Department of English at the University of California, Riverside, before which she was the co-founder and chair of Black Studies and Associate Professor of American Studies at Occidental College. She earned her B.A. in Women's Studies from Harvard University and her Ph.D. in Literature from Duke University. Her book, *Humane Insight: Looking at Images of African American Suffering and Death*, was published by the University of Illinois Press in 2015. It examines the history of visualized black suffering in African American liberation movements. Her current project, entitled "The Tyranny of Realism: Twenty-First Century Blackness and the Ends of Cinema," entails a formalist analysis of recent American and British Black films.

Stephen Casmier is Associate Professor of English at Saint Louis University. His research unites his interest in race theory with his background as a newspaper journalist and includes efforts to reconceptualize the history of the Black Arts movement and the effects of neoliberalism on contemporary Black literary criticism. His current work explores how African American writers stage the tension between journalism and fiction in their work through newspaper stories. His book manuscript (provisionally titled *Bewitching the Word: The Press, Race and African American Literature*) analyzes how African American novels and narratives confront what one historian calls the "fictiveness" of the daily newspaper, its construction of identity, and its support of racial hegemony.

Toni Pressley-Sanon is Associate Professor of Africology and African American Studies at Eastern Michigan University. She is the coeditor of *Raoul Peck: Power, Politics and the Cinematic Imagination* (Lexington Books, 2015) and the author of *Istwa across the Water: Haitian History,*

Memory, and the Cultural Imagination (University Press of Florida, 2017). She is also the author of numerous articles on Haitian literature, visual art, and film.

Laura Rascaroli is Professor of Film and Screen Media at the University College Cork, Ireland. Her interests span art film, modernism and postmodernism, geopolitics, nonfiction, first-person cinema, and the essay film. She is the author of several monographs, including *How the Essay Film Thinks* (Oxford University Press, 2017), *The Personal Camera: Subjective Cinema and the Essay Film* (Wallflower/Columbia University Press, 2009), and *Crossing New Europe: Postmodern Travel and the European Road Movie* (with Ewa Mazierska, Wallflower/Columbia University Press, 2006), and the editor of collections including *Antonioni: Centenary Essays* (with John David Rhodes, BFI, 2011). Her new collection, *Expanding Cinema: Theorizing Film through Contemporary Art*, coedited with Jill Murphy, is forthcoming in 2020. She is the general editor of *Alphaville: Journal of Film and Screen Media*.

Ellen C. Scott is Associate Professor and Vice Chair of Cinema and Media Studies in the Department of Film, Television and Digital Media at the University of California, Los Angeles. Her research focuses on the meanings and reverberations of film in African American communities. Her first book, *Cinema Civil Rights* (Rutgers, 2015), exposed the Classical Hollywood-era studio system's repression of civil rights issues but also their stuttered appearance through latent, symptomatic signifiers taken up by Black reviewers and activists. She recently guest edited a special issue of *Black Camera* entitled "Black Images Matter: Contextualizing Images of Racialized Police Violence" and is working on two book projects: "Cinema's Peculiar Institution," supported by an Academy Scholars grant, examines the history of slavery on the American screen and "Bitter Ironies, Tender Hopes" explores Classical Hollywood-era's Black women film critics.

Index

Note: Page numbers followed by "n" denote endnotes.

absence 10, 13, 21, 28, 31, 79
activism 1, 41–42, 44, 50
Acton, Jay 12, 18, 27
adaptation 15
Aggressives, The 19
Angelou, Maya 58, 59–61, 63–64, 68
Another Country 61
antiblackness 9, 13
archival images 2, 4, 6, 13, 26, 27, 29, 62, 83
archive 10, 11, 13–14, 21
Aristide, Jean-Bertrand 73
assemblage 4, 30, 65
Autobiography of Malcolm X, The 16

Badette, Laurette 77
Baker, Damani 42–43
Baker, Ella 40
Baraka, Amiri 58, 68
Barthes, Roland 11, 14, 15, 26, 31
Bishop, Maurice 42
Black Lives Matter 2, 29, 52, 62
Black men 38, 45, 48–49
Black nationalism 56, 59, 65
blackness 6, 9, 34; *see also* antiblackness
Black Power movement 29, 57, 64
Black women 38, 40–41, 42, 43, 45, 47, 50, 56
Bland, Edward 38
Bland, Sandra 38, 40
Bluest Eye, The 75
body 24–35, 44, 46–47, 48
Brown, Michael 38, 83

Buckley, William F. 4
Burnett, Charles 49

Carmichael, Stokely 58
Castile, Philando 38
Cavett, Dick 62–63, 80
cinema 4, 9, 27, 48
civil rights movement 17, 29, 34, 64, 77
Cleaver, Eldridge 61
Clinton, Bill 59
Collins, Kathleen 49–50
Combahee River Collective 40, 53, 56
cosmology (Black Atlantic and Haitian) 67–68
counterculture 56
Counts, Dorothy 41, 76
Cry of Jazz, The 38
culture wars 55, 57

"Damn Right, I've Got the Blues" (Buddy Guy) 12, 62
Davis, Angela 38, 42
Davis, Damani 48
Davis, Damon 48
Davis, Fania 42
Day, Doris 28, 29, 39, 76
Defiant Ones, The 18, 28
Deren, Maya 67–68
Desounen: Dialogue with Death 73, 81–83
Devil Finds Work, The 13, 14, 19, 27, 39
Dick Cavett Show, The 4, 11, 62–63, 75

documentary 5, 9, 15, 30, 38; *see also* experimental documentary
Douglass, Frederick 72, 74, 75
Duvalier, François (Papa Doc) 73, 77
Duvalier, Jean-Claude (Baby Doc) 73, 77

Elephant 65
embodiment 26, 29, 31–35
Epistemology of the Closet 60
essay film 4–5, 26, 30
Evers, Medgar 9, 17, 26, 27, 28, 29, 40, 45, 54, 64, 74
experimental documentary 44–48

Fatal Assistance 74
Ferguson 11–12, 39, 40, 41, 52, 62
Ferrell, Brittany 41–42
Fire Next Time, The 1
Folayan, Sabaah 48
Ford, Yance 38, 44–45, 48

Garner, Eric 38, 47
gender 40–41, 43–45, 47–50, 60
Giovanni's Room 49
Godard, Jean-Luc 29
Goldberg, Whoopi 47
Gospel According to St. Matthew, The 24–25
Go Tell It on the Mountain 61
Graham, Ramarley 38
Grant, Oscar 38
Gray, Freddie 38, 83
grief 44–45, 46
Grier, David Alan 59
Guess Who's Coming to Dinner 20–21, 28
Gunn, Bill 49
Guy, Buddy 12, 62

Haitian Corner 73, 76, 77, 81–82
Haitian Revolution 10, 75
Haitian Voudoun 67
Hamm, Jon 47
Hampton, Fred 53–54, 57, 69n6
Hansberry, Lorraine 28, 40–41, 45–47
Happersberger, Lucien 55, 61
Histoire(s) du cinema 29
history 5, 10, 27, 29, 53, 65–66, 67, 78; Marxist revisionist history 52, 54, 65; *see also* New Historicism

Hollywood 14, 16, 28, 29, 76
homophobia 46, 49, 56, 60
homosexuality 34, 45, 56
hooks, bell 49
Houghton, Fannie 42–43
Houghton, Katherine 20
House on Coco Road, The 42–44
Hughes, Langston 55
human rights 77, 83

identification 14, 18, 32, 33–34, 45, 49
identity 9, 10, 12, 17, 26, 48, 56; gay identity 34, 49, 60; intersectional approaches 41; lesbian identity 45–46; queer identity 9, 18, 19, 46, 60; transgender identity 44
identity politics 52, 53–54, 55–57, 63, 65–66
If Beale Street Could Talk 3
Imitation of Life 76
injustice 3, 5, 44, 72, 74
Intellettuale 24–26, 33, 35
In the Heat of the Night 19–21, 28
invisibility 21, 27

Jackson, Jesse 54, 56–57
Jackson, Samuel L. 12, 16, 27, 30–32, 63–64, 65, 81
James Baldwin: The Price of the Ticket 7, 52, 54–55, 57–61, 62, 63, 65–66, 68
Jenkins, Barry 3
Jones, Aiyana Mo'Nay Stanley 83

Karefa-Smart, Gloria 64
Keeling, Kara 13–14, 17, 19
Kennedy, Bobby 40
Kennedy, John F. 74
Kerouac, Jack 25–26
King, Jr., Martin Luther 9, 17, 26, 27, 28, 29, 40, 45, 54, 63, 64, 65, 74
King, Rodney 29

Lacks, Henrietta 40
Lane, Charles 49
Lee, Spike 49
Looking for Langston 55, 60
Lorraine Hansberry: Sighted Eyes/Feeling Heart 45–46
Lover Come Back 29, 76

Lubiano, Wahneemah 49
Lumumba 73
Lumumba: Death of a Prophet (Lumumba: la mort du prophète) 10, 11, 13, 66, 73, 78, 81
Lumumba, Patrice 73, 78–79

Malcolm X 9, 16, 17, 26, 27, 28, 29, 40, 42, 45, 46–47, 52, 54, 62, 64, 65, 74, 75
Man by the Shore, The 73, 81, 82
masculinity 34–35, 41, 42, 45, 48
Masotti, Antonio 24–25
Mauri, Fabio 24–26
McBride, Renisha 38
McDonald, Laquan 38
memoir 14, 27, 54
memory 14
Mitchell, Charlene 42
Moloch Tropical 73, 80
montage 11, 16, 29, 43, 62, 80, 81–82
Morrison, Toni 58, 72–73, 75, 79
mourning 13
multiculturalism 55
Murder in Pacot 74, 80
The Murder of Fred Hampton 69n6
myth 11, 30

Nance, Terrance 47–48
narration 14, 15, 31, 47
Nelson, Laura 76
New Historicism 52–53, 66
New Jewel movement 42
No Name in the Street 27

Obama, Barack 2, 3
OJ: Made in America 1
Ové, Horace 4
Oversimplification of Her Beauty, An 47

Pajama Game, The 38
Parks, Gordon 58
Pasolini, Pier Paolo 24–26, 33, 35
poetics 9, 11, 13, 14, 15
Poitier, Sidney 19–21, 28
police violence 1, 26, 29, 49
Profit and Nothing But! Or Impolite Thoughts on the Class Struggle 73, 81
progressiveness 9
Prophete, Denise 77

queerness 17–18, 19, 34, 39; James Baldwin's queer identity 9, 18, 21n1, 34, 42, 56, 60; queer body 26, 33, 35

race 9, 18, 34, 50, 53, 67
racism 3, 15, 39, 40, 46, 49, 78
Rainbow Coalition 53–54, 56–57
Random Acts of Flyness 47–48
Reagan, Ronald 42, 43, 56
recovery 52–54, 55, 57, 59, 62, 65, 67
Remember This House 12, 13, 14, 17, 27, 48, 54, 64, 74, 79
revolution 41, 42, 43, 45, 50
Rice, Tamir 11, 38, 83
Roach, Max 58–59
Robeson, Eslanda 40

School Daze 49
Scott, Walter 11, 38, 83
sexism 46, 83
sexuality 44, 48, 49, 60; James Baldwin's sexuality 18–19, 34–35, 42, 63
She's Gotta Have It 47, 49
slavery 72, 74
Smith, Anthony Lamar 38
social justice 72, 74, 83
Sometimes in April 73, 80
Soul on Ice 61
Steiger, Rod 19–21
Strain, Tracey Heather 45–46, 48
Strauss, Alexandra 31, 65
Strong Island 38, 44–45, 46

tableau vivant 80, 81–83, 85n37
Take This Hammer 4
Taylor, Clyde 58
Technicolor 28, 38
temporality 4, 6; queer temporality 17–18
testimony 30, 77, 81
Thorsen, Karen 52, 54–55
time 4, 59, 10, 12, 16, 19
timeliness 2, 3–5
Tonton Macoutes 77, 81, 85n25
Trump, Donald 1, 3, 39
truth-telling 72, 73, 74, 79
Turner, Nat 75

Uptown Young Patriots 57
utterance 9, 31

violence 29, 39, 76, 77, 80, 83
voice 12, 28, 30–32, 47–48, 59; James Baldwin's voice 30–32, 41, 46, 52, 59–60; Maya Angelou's voice 59–60; Samuel L. Jackson's voice 30–32, 63–64
voice-over 30–32, 80–81, 85n37

Washington, Booker T. 14
Wayne, John 16

West, Cornel 72, 74
whiteness 27, 39, 48
white supremacy 2, 13, 39, 44, 48, 72, 83
Whose Streets? 41–42, 44, 45
witness 17–18, 45; bearing witness 72, 74, 77–78, 79
women *see* Black women

Yevtushenko, Yevgeny 25
The Young Karl Marx 84n9, 85n37

For Product Safety Concerns and Information please contact our EU representative GPSR@taylorandfrancis.com
Taylor & Francis Verlag GmbH, Kaufingerstraße 24, 80331 München, Germany

www.ingramcontent.com/pod-product-compliance
Lightning Source LLC
Chambersburg PA
CBHW070740230426
43669CB00014B/2527